Mother
& Child Companion

MQ Publications Limited
12 The Ivories, 6–8 Northampton Street
London N1 2HY
Tel: +44 (0) 20 7359 2244
Fax: +44 (0) 20 7359 1616
email: mail@mqpublications.com
www.mqpublications.com

ISBN: 1-84072-777-2

10 9 8 7 6 5 4 3 2 1

Printed and bound in China

Mother
& Child Companion

KATE ASHTON

MQP

Contents

6 Introduction • **8** Home at last! • **12** *Madame Bovary* • **18** Cradle and all • **20** Introducing the new baby! • **22** *Baby* • **26** Mother's milk • **30** Bottle-feeding the baby • **32** Glowing with health! • **34** Soft and white, so eco-right! • **36** Baby on wheels • **38** And baby goes too… • **40** My little spring lamb • **42** *The Light Princess* • **50** One step, two step… • **52** *I'm From…* • **54** Bath time fun • **56** Toothy, toothy tiger • **58** Time for bed • **60** *All Through the Night* • **64** Lullabies • **70** Please, give me sleep! • **74** Oh those baby blues! • **76** *Anne of Green Gables* • **82** The Great Mother • **86** The godmother • **88** *The Child's Quest* • **90** How does it grow? • **92** Eggheads • **98** I can dress myself • **102** You're a big person now! • **104** Bigger and better every day • **106** Togetherness • **110** Food, glorious food! • **112** Ma's magic chicken noodle soup with vegetables • **116** Mother's trying to talk! • **118** *The Chatterbox* • **122** Swing high, swing low! • **124** Come fly my kite • **126** Flying fish kite • **130** Fun by the sea… • **132** Seaside picnic • **136** *American Woman's Home* • **146** *Pat-a-cake* • **148** Mother's baking tips • **150** Mama's magic apple pie • **152** Look after yourself! • **156** Pet loves • **160** Mother Goose • **164** What shall we read? • **166**

Reading together • **168** *Little Women* • **174** With a wave of a wand… • **176** The dress-up box • **180** Making music • **184** Water xylophone • **190** Clap hands and dance • **192** Laundry day • **196** Working mothers • **198** *There Was An Old Woman* • **200** Playing mother • **202** *Snow White* • **206** Mother's Day • **208** Homemade lemonade • **210** Hot chocolate • **212** Shy baby! • **214** Safe with mother • **216** Just you and me • **220** Head nurse • **224** Can I get into your bed? • **226** Sad and blue • **228** *Prelude* • **232** I'll whisper it • **234** Like mother, like daughter • **236** The gentle touch • **238** One at a time… • **242** *Pride and Prejudice* • **246** A room of one's own • **248** Fat cat doorstop • **252** Run and get… • **254** Shopping savvy • **256** Trick or treat? • **258** Halloween jack o'lantern • **262** Halloween pumpkin pie • **264** The A-Team • **268** Wish you were here • **272** *See-saw, Margery Daw* • **274** Toys, glorious toys! • **276** A puppet to play • **280** First snow • **282** Mother Christmas • **284** Gingerbread Christmas cookies • **286** Christmas tree fairy • **292** Party animals • **296** Then there's the sleepover… • **298** Watch the birdie! • **300** *Alice's Adventures in Wonderland* • **304** Picture Credits

Introduction

You may have often thrown up your hands in exasperation and said, "Who'd be a mother?" Well, here's the answer! After all those years of patient nurturing, now it's your time to stop and take a moment to reflect upon what it all means. You deserve this little luxury, so sit down in your favorite chair and enjoy the pleasure of contemplating all you have achieved. Here in the pages of the *Mother and Child Companion* you will find a wonderful celebration of all your own precious moments as a mother.

A lovingly composed homage to mothering, the *Mother and Child Companion* provides a treasure trove of famous and less famous words, poems, pictures, and rhymes to express the joy and sometimes the anguish of motherhood, encompassing both its universality and its uniqueness. For although babies are born everywhere, every minute, your baby is the most beautiful, the most gifted, the most entrancing. The timeless and tender illustrations throughout the book perfectly evoke the atmosphere of mothering and childhood in its own landscape of love.

The *Mother and Child Companion* will provide hours of private and shared pleasure: a source of smiles, hints, tips, history, and useful things to know. Find a favorite recipe and lovely things to make together. Learn how to fly a kite, grow a cress caterpillar or make bubbles. Discover truths about diapers and baby carriages and what to do when nobody can get to sleep! And how mothers used to cope a hundred years ago—a potpourri of common sense and comfort, balm for your busy soul!

The *Mother and Child Companion* is a book for every mother—and every mother to be! It's a book of memories, of inspiration and everlasting hope—in fact, a perfect companion. Give it, hold it for yourself, or share it with those you love and who in gratitude love you.

Home at last!

After all the months of preparation, hours spent decorating the nursery, all the anticipation—and finally, all the real-life drama of giving birth—at last mother brings baby home from the maternity ward. But what does home mean to baby? It's father's proud, beaming face and the excited shouts of big brother and sister. It's grandmother's gentle arms, and grandfather's tender admiration. Mostly, though, it is mother.

Home is a freshly painted nursery, a lace-draped crib, the smell of fresh bedsheets, a nest of softest eiderdown. It is the tinkling sound when a bright mobile moves, light playing on the ceiling, the smell of milk and soap and warm, soft skin. It is mother.

Home is the place where you are the most important person in the world because you are the newest. And everyone coos and oohs and says you're so sweet and cute and utterly adorable, as they bring you teddy bears and dolls and cuddly toys. But all you really want to hold is mother. Home is made of smiles and tears; of windows where the moon peeps in, and new faces and new little fears. Finally, home is where you're warm and safe and loved just because you're you.

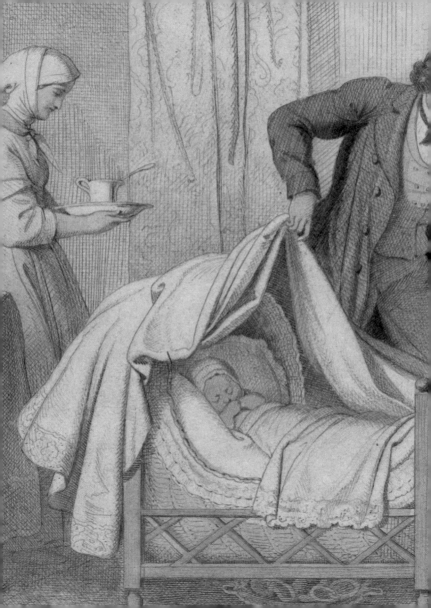

It sometimes happens, even in the best of families, that a baby is born. This is not necessarily cause for alarm. The important thing is to keep your wits about you and borrow some money.

ELINOR GOULDING SMITH

Madame Bovary

by

GUSTAVE FLAUBERT

Emma at first felt a great astonishment; then was anxious to be delivered that she might know what it was to be a mother. But not being able to spend as much as she would have liked, to have a swing-bassinette with rose silk curtains, and embroidered caps, in a fit of bitterness she gave up looking after the trousseau, and ordered the whole of it from a village needlewoman, without choosing or discussing anything. Thus she did not amuse herself with those preparations that stimulate the tenderness of mothers, and so her affection was from the very outset, perhaps, to some extent attenuated.

As Charles, however, spoke of the boy at every meal, she soon began to think of him more consecutively.

She hoped for a son; he would be strong and dark; she would call him George; and this idea of having a male child was like an expected revenge for all her impotence in the past. A man, at least, is free; he may travel over passions and over countries, overcome obstacles, taste of the most far-away pleasures. But a woman is always hampered. At once inert and flexible, she has against her the weakness of the flesh and legal dependence. Her will, like the veil of her bonnet, held by a string, flutters in every wind; there is always some desire that draws her, some conventionality that restrains.

She was confined on a Sunday at about six o'clock, as the sun was rising.

"It is a girl!" said Charles.

She turned her head away and fainted.

... Monsieur Bovary, senior, stayed at Yonville a month, dazzling the native by a superb policeman's cap with silver tassels that he wore in the morning when he smoked his pipe in the square. Being also in the habit of drinking a good deal of brandy, he often sent the servant to the Lion d'Or to buy him a bottle, which was put down to his son's account, and to perfume his handkerchiefs he used up his daughter-in-law's whole supply of eau-de-cologne.

The latter did not at all dislike his company. He had knocked about the world, he talked about Berlin, Vienna, and Strasbourg, of his soldier times, of the mistresses he had had, the grand luncheons of which he had partaken; then he was amiable, and sometimes even, either on the stairs, or in the garden, would seize hold of her waist, crying, "Charles, look out for yourself."

Then Madame Bovary, senior, became alarmed for her son's happiness, and fearing that her husband might in the long-run have an immoral influence upon the ideas of the young woman, took care to hurry their departure. Perhaps she had more serious reasons for uneasiness. Monsieur Bovary was not the man to respect anything.

One day Emma was suddenly seized with the desire to see her little girl, who had been put to nurse with the carpenter's wife, and, without looking at the calendar to see whether the six weeks of the Virgin were yet passed, she set out for the Rollets' ☞

house, situated at the extreme end of the village, between the highroad and the fields.

It was mid-day, the shutters of the houses were closed and the slate roofs that glittered beneath the fierce light of the blue sky seemed to strike sparks from the crest of the gables. A heavy wind was blowing; Emma felt weak as she walked; the stones of the pavement hurt her; she was doubtful whether she would not go home again, or go in somewhere to rest.

At this moment Monsieur Leon came out from a neighboring door with a bundle of papers under his arm. He came to greet her, and stood in the shade in front of the Lheureux's shop under the projecting grey awning.

Madame Bovary said she was going to see her baby, but that she was beginning to grow tired.

"If—" said Leon, not daring to go on.

"Have you any business to attend to?" she asked.

And on the clerk's answer, she begged him to accompany her. That same evening this was known in Yonville, and Madame Tuvache, the mayor's wife, declared in the presence of her servant that "Madame Bovary was compromising herself."

To get to the nurse's it was necessary to turn to the left on leaving the street, as if making for the cemetery, and to follow between little houses and yards a small path bordered with privet hedges. They were in bloom, and so were the speedwells, eglantines, thistles, and the sweetbriar that sprang up from the thickets. Through openings in the hedges one could see into the huts, some pigs on a dung-heap, or tethered cows rubbing their horns against the trunk of trees. The two, side by side, walked slowly, she leaning upon him, and he restraining his pace, which he regulated by hers; in front of them a swarm of midges fluttered, buzzing in the warm air.

The recognized the house by an old walnut-tree which shaded it.

Low and covered with brown tiles, there hung outside it, beneath the dormer-window of the garret, a string of onions. Faggots upright against a thorn fence surrounded a bed of lettuce, a few square feet of lavender, and sweet peas strung on sticks. Dirty water was running here and there on the grass, and all round were several indefinite rags, knitted stockings, a red calico jacket, and a large sheet of coarse linen spread over the hedge. At the noise of the gate the nurse appeared with a baby she was suckling on one arm. With her other hand she was pulling along a poor puny little fellow, his face covered with scrofula, the son of a Rouen hosier, whom his parents, too taken up with their business, left in the country.

"Go in," she said, "your little one is there asleep."

The room on the ground-floor, the only one in the dwelling, had at its farther end, against the wall, a large bed without curtains, while a kneading-trough took up the side by the window, one pane of which was mended with a piece of blue paper. In the corner behind the door, shining hob-nailed shoes stood in a row under the slab of the washstand, near a bottle

☞ of oil with a feather stuck in its mouth; a Matthieu Laensberg lay on the dusty mantelpiece amid gunflints, candle-ends, and bits of amadou.

Finally, the last luxury in the apartment was a "Fame" blowing her trumpets, a picture cut out, no doubt, from some perfumer's prospectus and nailed to the wall with six wooden shoe-pegs.

Emma's child was asleep in a wicker-cradle. She took it up in the wrapping that enveloped it and began singing softly as she rocked herself to and fro.

Leon walked up and down the room; it seemed strange to him to see this beautiful woman in her nankeen dress in the midst of all this poverty. Madame Bovary reddened; he turned away, thinking perhaps there had been an impertinent look in his eyes. Then she put back the little girl, who had just been sick over her collar.

The nurse at once came to dry her, protesting that it wouldn't show.

"She gives me other doses," she said, "I am always a-washing of her. If you would have the goodness to order Camus, the grocer, to let me have a little soap, it would really be more convenient for you, as I needn't trouble you then."

"Very well! Very well!" said Emma. "Good morning, Madame Rollet," and she went out, wiping her shoes at the door.

The good woman accompanied her to the end of the garden, talking all the time of the trouble she had getting up of nights.

"I'm that worn out sometimes as I drop asleep on my chair. I'm sure you might at least give me just a pound of ground coffee; that'd last me a month, and I'd take it of a morning with some milk."

After having submitted to her thanks, Madame Bovary left. She had gone a little way down the path when, at the sound of wooden shoes, she turned round. It was the nurse.

"What is it?"

Then the peasant woman, taking her aside behind an elm tree, began talking to her of her husband, who with his trade and six francs a year that the captain—

"Oh, be quick!" said Emma.

"Well," the nurse went on, heaving sighs between each word, "I'm afraid he'll be put out seeing me have coffee along, you know men—"

"But you are to have some," Emma repeated; "I will give you some. You bother me!"

"Oh, dear! My poor, dear lady! You see in consequence of his wounds he has terrible cramps in the chest. He even says that cider weakens him."

"Do make haste, Mère Rollet!"

"Well," the latter continued, making a curtsey, "if it weren't asking too much," and she curtsied once more, "if you would"— and her eyes begged—"a jar of brandy," she said at last, "and I'd rub your little one's feet with it; they're as tender as one's tongue."

CRADLE AND ALL

One of the nicest parts of preparing for a new baby is choosing a crib or cradle. Many mothers invest a great deal of creativity in this choice. An old wickerwork crib can be painted, using non-toxic paint, and beautified with freshly sewn frills and curtains, or you can paint a wooden crib with colors that match the baby's room. Last-minute postnatal additions of suitable ribbons complete the job. With just a little love and imagination, you can turn a rocking cradle or Moses basket from a thrift store or grandmother's attic into a uniquely adorable bed for the new baby.

There is a sort of continuity in a mother's revamping of the crib rather than buying it new, because she has been her baby's cradle up until the birth. Babies are rocked in the womb, to the rhythm of the mother's heartbeat, and by three months' gestation, their balancing mechanism is already established. They also tune in to various maternal internal processes—a kind of rehearsal for "Listen with Mother." So a rocking cradle and a cradle song, combined with a full stomach and a clean diaper, are guaranteed to lull baby to sleep. It was the French physician LeBoyer, the modern-day advocate of natural childbirth, who recommended that babies be comforted by such soothing conditions. A cradle should rock on an axis with the baby's center of gravity, so the baby rocks rather than swings. Finally, the crib needs to be big enough to last until the child is about a year old. By that time, baby will need a bed. But that is a rite of passage to another era, for along with the crib, babyhood itself is left behind.

Introducing the new baby!

Whether the news is conveyed in a "new baby" greeting card or a box in the community newspaper, the arrival of a baby is an important event everywhere! And there are so many different ways of spreading the word. In Greece, gifts of silver or gold coins are bestowed upon the newborn; this is to *asimo to pethi* or "silver the child." Other gifts may be given to ward off the "evil eye," such as a mati, a small blue stone with a black eye, or a small pouch of sacred items. Earlier generations are honored in the choosing of names.

The placing of branches at the left of the doorway announces the birth of a boy among the Sha people of Yunnan province in China. The branches signify three things: the joy of the parents, a warning that people may not enter, and that the mother and child must be protected. No man is allowed to enter the mother's home for three days after the birth, including the father of the child.

Sikh boy children must carry the name Singh. As soon after the birth as the mother can walk and take a bath, the family and relatives must go with a sacred sweetmeat to the gurdwara, or temple, and recite hymns of thanksgiving in front of the Guru Granth Sahib, the Sikh holy book.

The first voice a Moslem baby hears is that of the father or nearest male relative, who whispers the *adhan*, or call to prayer, first into his right ear and then into the left.

According to Hindu mythology, the mainly ladies-only naming ceremony for a newborn takes place on the twelfth day after a birth. The newborn is placed in a jhula, or cradle, decorated with colorful flowers and ribbons, and all the women gather around it, singing traditional ceremonial songs that rhyme with the baby's name.

Amongst the Nandis of the Great Rift Valley in Africa, naming takes place in the mother's hut while the men wait outside, not yet having been told the sex of the child. The name of a spirit is called to watch over the child and the baby is supposed to sneeze to indicate acceptance of the name. Snuff "helps" the baby choose its name and from the intervals between the women's gales of laughter, the men outside are supposed to guess whether it is a boy or a girl.

To announce a birth in China, parents send red eggs to family and friends —an even number for a girl, odd for a boy. It is considered unlucky to think of a name before the child is born; false or "milk" names are given to scare away evil spirits.

In Malaysia, every new life is seen as a carrier of light, so a bright light burns day and night in the baby's home for the first forty days. The baby is introduced first to the grandparents, to honor them. But however universal the good tidings, every new mother feels as if she is the first and only and luckiest mother in the world!

Baby

Where did you come from baby dear?

Out of the everywhere into here.

Where did you get those eyes so blue?

Out of the sky as I came through.

What makes the light in them sparkle and spin?

Some of the starry twinkles left in.

Where did you get that little tear?

I found it waiting when I got here.

What makes your forehead so smooth and high?

A soft hand stroked it as I went by.

What makes your cheek like a warm white rose?

I saw something better than anyone knows.

Whence that three-cornered smile of bliss?

Three Angels gave me at once a kiss.

Where did you get this pearly ear?

God spoke and it came out to hear.

Where did you get those arms and hands?

Love made itself into bonds and bands.

Feet, whence did you come, you darling things?

From the same box as the cherub's wings.

How did they all just come to be you?

God thought about me, and so I grew.

But how did you come to us, you dear?

God thought about you, and so I'm here.

GEORGE MACDONALD

Where did you come
from baby dear?

Mother's milk

Who fed me from her gentle breast
And hushed me in her arms to rest?

ANN TAYLOR

Breastfeeding gives mother and child the chance to get to know each other in ways that will last a lifetime. The "skin to skin" intimacy may take the new mother completely by surprise as she meets her child's steady gaze and feels little fingers stroking her. She's her child's first toy—and while she may feel amazed at it all, her baby seems perfectly at home.

Breast milk is true convenience food and a perfect product. It comes on demand: sterile, perfectly balanced, with nutritional value added according to the client's needs, in client-centered volume. It's fast and it's ready-warmed. What more could either of you want? Well, okay, you could sometimes want to go out and leave the feeding to someone else, but that's what breast pumps are for. Breast milk can be frozen so that baby still gets the best.

Breast-feeding is, of course, the natural way, but like everything else in motherhood, it has to be learned. No first-time mother should ever feel ashamed to ask advice from a health professional rather than give up. "Breast is best."

A mother passes on her immunities to her child through her breast milk, so a breast-fed infant develops a healthier immune system than does a bottle-fed child. And because human milk is perfectly adjusted to the human digestive tract, the breast-fed child also suffers far less from colic and intestinal upsets.

Detail of a mother nursing her baby on an Etruscan-style Sèvres vase made in 1827–1832. The vase was modeled by Percier and painted by Beranger.

BOTTLE-FEEDING THE BABY

Mothers who decide to bottle-feed face a mind-boggling choice of fabricated milk formulas. If in doubt, it's probably best to consult a pediatrician for advice on which will best suit baby. Formulas are made up from cow's milk or soy solution, and fortified with a range of additives to boost the nutritional content baby's getting.

The upside of bottle-feeding is that you don't always have to be there. The downside is that formula does not come baby-ready. It is sold mostly as powder or concentrate that has to be diluted with water, put into a sterile bottle with a sterile nipple, then carefully warmed to the correct temperature. By this stage in the proceedings, baby is probably squalling with hunger rage, while the preparation hassles are no doubt taking their toll on mother too. The smartest way to avoid stress of this sort is to feed on demand rather than trying to stick to a rigid schedule.

The golden rule seems to be that junior knows best. And this goes for the choice of formula too. It soon becomes evident that whichever brand suits baby's digestive system is also best for baby's mood and, by extrapolation, for mother's. A baby should be nursed comfortably in the crook of mother's arm. It is not a good idea to give a bottle to a baby who's lying down.

The crucially important technique to learn is "winding" the bottle-fed baby—it's essential, as air swallowed because the nipple isn't constantly filled with milk during the feeding accumulates in baby's stomach, leaving no room for any more formula. Every two ounces is the best burping interval. This way the formula should remain in situ and mother's "burping" shoulder will stay clean and dry.

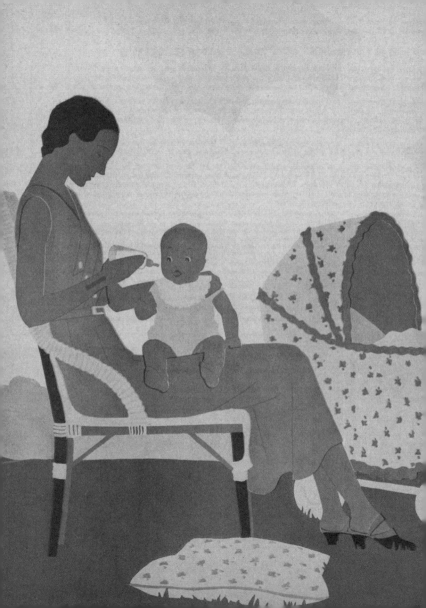

It's a very odd thing—
As odd as can be—
That whatever Miss T eats
Turns into Miss T.

WALTER DE LA MARE

Glowing with health!

When it comes to eating and drinking, mother knows what is best for baby—she knows he has to triple his weight in the first year. The trouble is, baby also knows what is best for him. Once the joys of breast- or bottle-feeding make way for the plate and spoon, a whole new universe of interaction opens up between mother and child. It's time to see who is boss.

Now, mother knows that her baby needs milk, grains, fruit, delicious, healthy vegetables, and a little meat. Having lovingly peeled and prepared these goodies; cooked, mashed, or blended them, and put them in baby's favorite little bowl with the special rabbit picture on it, she lifts baby into the highchair. She puts a bib around the infant's neck and fills the spoon, tries it to see if it's too hot, and enthuses, "Ooo, that tastes REALLY good!"

Baby is not impressed. Mother spoons it in; he spits it out. She spoons it in again; he spits with more conviction. This time she has to scoop and spoon and then retrieve the overflow from baby's chin. He regards her efforts with the utmost impassivity, merely purses his lips a little tighter and at the next spoonful turns his face suddenly and smartly away. She tries "the train going into the tunnel"…choo, choo! Spit…And "the big airplane coming in to land"…wheeeee! Spit.

Is he really not hungry? Well, by now she certainly is! And that's how mother triples her own weight, while her child, smiling happily at the clinic doctor, stays right on target.

Soft and white, so eco-right!

The sight of a new mother hanging out cloth diapers in the sunshine used to be one of the nicest in the neighborhood. A clothesline full of bright, new, white diapers blowing in the breeze told of her happiness and pride better than any words could communicate. And when they were dry, she'd bring them in, fold them neatly, and pile them in the baby's dresser.

As if to compensate for the threadbare state of the postwar world into which they were born, some baby boomers wore deliciously luxurious, Turkish cotton terry-towel diapers. Scented with soap and fresh air, these were folded into a kite shape with the "tail" folded upward again to make a double thickness. Baby was then placed with his or her waist over the "base" of the triangle, the doubled-over tail drawn up between the legs and the other two points of the triangle secured to it with a safety pin—so-named because it had a baby-proof lock top that hid the sharp point.

In 1950, an intrepid young American mother called Marion Donovan invented the earliest version of today's disposable, and waterproof, diaper. These are now universally popular, of course! Every baby is estimated to use two tons of diapers during babyhood, and each diaper takes approximately 500 years to break down in a landfill. Consequently, many eco-aware mothers are choosing "real" diapers again. But today they are shaped to fit well, and are less likely to cause diaper rash.

Baby on wheels

Wheeling out baby for the first time is a special moment for the new mother. It can also be pretty nerve-racking to be in charge of a stroller or baby carriage on busy streets full of traffic. But once used to the novel experience, most mothers enjoy showing off baby. The public response is amazing. When you're used to walking sedately and anonymously alone, it comes as quite a surprise to be addressed by perfect strangers, who peep into the carriage and shower baby with compliments.

William Kent, an English garden architect, designed the first known baby carriage for the third Duke of Devonshire in 1733. It was shell-shaped, spring-sprung, and could be harnessed to a goat! The wealthy classes of Europe soon adopted this new fad, their little carriages being pulled by ponies before the handle finally evolved.

In 1840 Queen Victoria herself ordered three baby carriages, or "perambulators," and in 1889, the American William Richardson revolutionized the design by turning the carriage around so the occupant faced the person pushing it. By the end of the First World War, almost everyone could afford a baby carriage, and by then brakes and rubber wheels had been added.

The next leap forward came with the British aeronautical engineer Owen Maclaren in 1965: he designed an aluminum-framed stroller for his grandson—the light, strong, foldable forerunner of the modern stroller. Today, strollers come in all kinds of designs and colors—and there's considerable competition between fashionable mothers to see who's wheeling out the latest model. As for babies? They just enjoy being wheeled around and admired.

And baby goes too ...

All over the world mothers have improvised ways of carrying their children so that they can conduct their normal work relatively unhampered. Most carriers, like the *reobozo* or shawl traditionally used by Mexican women, are of simple design and strong fabric. Traditionally, Japanese babies were carried on their mother's back in the sash of her kimono, then in an *onbuhimo*, a cozy cloth carrier.

Whatever the origins of today's baby carriers, it is the loveliest feeling to have your baby's body close to your own while you're walking. The idea is to sling baby in any one of various positions, keeping him or her safe and near, and lulled by your heartbeat—the familiar sound baby danced and slept to in your womb. It's also a perfect way for fathers to carry babies around!

Many modern pouches based on ethnic designs are "front" carriers in which the baby travels facing you, with knees pulled up at an optimum 45 degrees. This is very convenient because you can converse, or baby can sleep, as required. Also, breast-feeding is easy and private, because the carrier can fit under a coat.

Close contact between infant and mother is known to be highly beneficial, and there is even evidence to suggest that it has an enhancing effect on babies' intelligence. But this centuries-old method really comes into its own when baby is a few months old. If crying from the nursery signals that baby's woken up, a handy baby carrier is a "hands-free" way of getting everything done, and there are no wheels you have to navigate up or down the stairs.

My little spring lamb

As the smiling springtime's
Fairest charm.

GOETHE

March, April, and May are the loveliest months in which to become a
mother. Everything in nature is being reborn just as you have your baby.
In city parks the birds start to sing a different song, and fresh, green
leaves sparkle in the sunshine. In the fields, lambs frisk and kneel and
pester the patient ewes. Daffodils break out of bud, and in March the
cherry blossom bursts forth, frothing the trees with pink and white. In
Chinese and Japanese culture, this is the symbol of education and of
feminine dominance, the perfect expression of motherhood, with all its
strength and beauty.

A child born at this time of year is in complete harmony with the
natural cycle of the seasons, and mother and child are in tune with
eternal legend. The mystery of spring was enshrined in the Romano-
British spring celebrations held in April, called Eostermonat, as reported
by the Venerable Bede in the seventh century. Bede may have mixed the
April festival and the name of Eostre (probably goddess of spring or the
dawn), the Germanic version meaning "movement towards the rising
sun." But her true name might have been lost in translating the "rising of
the sap" festival into Latin, probably before the Roman legions left in the
fifth century. In Anglo-Saxon, her name became Estre or Eastre, which
survives today in our own festival of rebirth of life and nature after the
long winter months. So much mystery, but none so great as the wonder
of a new life.

The Light Princess

by

GEORGE MACDONALD

What! No Children?

Once upon a time, so long ago that I have quite forgotten the date, there lived a king and queen who had no children.

And the king said to himself, "All the queens of my acquaintance have children, some three, some seven, and some as many as twelve; and my queen has not one. I feel ill-used." So he made up his mind to be cross with his wife about it. But she bore it all like a good patient queen as she was. Then the king grew very cross indeed. But the queen pretended to take it all as a joke, and a very good one too.

"Why don't you have any daughters, at least?" said he. "I don't say sons; that might be too much to expect."

"I am sure, dear king, I am very sorry," said the queen.

"So you ought to be," retorted the king; "you are not going to make a virtue of that, surely."

But he was not an ill-tempered king, and in any matter of less moment would have let the queen have her own way with all his heart. This, however, was an affair of state.

The queen smiled.

"You must have patience with a lady, you know, dear king," said she.

She was, indeed, a very nice queen, and heartily sorry that she could not oblige the king immediately.

Won't I, Just?

The king tried to have patience, but he succeeded very badly. It was more than he deserved, therefore, when, at last, the queen gave him a daughter—as lovely a little princess as ever cried.

The day drew near when the infant must be christened. The king wrote all the invitations with his own hand. Of course somebody was forgotten. Now it does not generally matter if somebody is forgotten, only you must mind who. Unfortunately, the king forgot without intending to forget; and so the chance fell upon the Princess Makemnoit, which was awkward. For the princess was the king's own sister; and he ought not to have forgotten her. But she had made herself so disagreeable to the old king, their father, that he had forgotten her in making his will; and so it was no wonder that her brother forgot her in writing his invitations. But poor relations don't do anything to keep you in mind of them. Why don't they? The king could not see into the garret she lived in, could he?

She was a sour, spiteful creature. The wrinkles of contempt crossed the wrinkles of peevishness, and made her face as full of wrinkles as a pat of butter. If ever a king could be justified in forgetting anybody, this king was justified ☞

 in forgetting his sister, even at a christening. She looked very odd, too. Her forehead was as large as all the rest of her face, and projected over it like a precipice. When she was angry, her little eyes flashed blue. When she hated anybody, they shone yellow and green. What they looked like when she loved anybody, I do not know; for I never heard of her loving anybody but herself and I do not think she could have managed that if she had not somehow got used to herself. But what made it highly imprudent in the king to forget her was that she was awfully clever. In fact, she was a witch; and when she bewitched anybody, he very soon had enough of it; for she beat all the wicked fairies in wickedness, and all the clever ones in cleverness. She despised all the modes we read of in history, in which offended fairies and witches have taken their revenges; and therefore, after waiting and waiting in vain for an invitation, she made up her mind at last to go without one, and make the whole family miserable, like a princess as she was.

So she put on her best gown, went to the palace, was kindly received by the happy monarch, who forgot that he had forgotten her, and took her place in the procession to the royal chapel. When they were all gathered about the font, she contrived to get next to it, and throw something into the water; after which she maintained a very respectful demeanour till the water was applied to the child's face. But at that moment she turned round in her place three

times, and muttered the following words, loud enough for those beside her to hear:

"Light of spirit, by my charms,
Light of body, every part,
Never weary human arms—
Only crush thy parents' heart!"

They all thought she had lost her wits, and was repeating some foolish nursery rhyme; but a shudder went through the whole of them notwithstanding. The baby, on the contrary, began to laugh and crow; while the nurse gave a start and a smothered cry, for she thought she was struck with paralysis: she could not feel the baby in her arms. But she clasped it tight and said nothing. The mischief was done.

She Can't Be Ours.

Her atrocious aunt had deprived the child of all her gravity. If you ask me how this was effected, I answer, "In the easiest way in the world. She had only to destroy gravitation." For the princess was a philosopher, and knew all the ins and outs of the laws of gravitation as well as the ins and outs of her boot-lace. And being a witch as well, she could abrogate those laws in a moment; or at least so clog their wheels and rust their bearings that they would not work at all. But we have more to do with what followed than with how it was done.

The first awkwardness that resulted from this unhappy privation was that the moment the nurse began to float the baby up and down, she flew from her arms towards the ceiling. Happily, the resistance of the air brought her ascending career to a close within a foot of it. There she remained, horizontal as when she left her nurse's arms, kicking and laughing amazingly. The nurse in terror flew to the bell, and begged the footman, who answered it, to bring up the house-steps directly. Trembling in every limb, she climbed upon the steps, and had to stand upon the very top, and reach up, before she could catch the floating tail of the baby's long clothes.

When the strange fact came to be known, there was a terrible commotion in the palace. The occasion of its discovery by the king was naturally a repetition of the nurse's experience. Astonished that he felt no weight when the child was laid in his arms, he began to wave her up and not down, for she slowly ascended to the ceiling as before, and there remained floating in perfect comfort and satisfaction, as was testified by her peals of tiny laughter. The king stood staring up in speechless amazement, and trembled so that his beard shook like grass in the wind. At last, turning to the queen, who was just as horror-struck as himself, he said, gasping, staring, and stammering,—

"She can't be ours, queen!"

Now the queen was much cleverer than the king, and had begun already to suspect that "this effect defective came by cause."

"I am sure she is ours," answered she. "But we ought to have taken better care of her at the christening. People who were never invited ought not to have been present."

"Oh, ho!" said the king, tapping his forehead with his forefinger, "I have it all. I've found her out. Don't you see it, queen? Princess Makemnoit has bewitched her."

"That's just what I say," answered the queen.

"I beg your pardon, my love; I did not hear you. John! Bring the steps I get on my throne with."

For he was a little king with a great throne, like many other kings.

The throne-steps were brought, and set upon the dining-table, and John got upon the top of them. But he could not reach the little princess, who lay like a baby-laughter-cloud in the air, exploding continuously. "Take the tongs, John," said his Majesty; and getting up on the table, he handed them to him.

John could reach the baby now, and the little princess was handed down by the tongs.

Where Is She?

One fine summer day, a month after these her first adventures, during which time she had been very carefully watched, the princess was lying on the bed in the queen's own chamber, fast asleep. One of the windows was open, for it was noon, and the day was so sultry that the little girl was ☞

wrapped in nothing less ethereal than slumber itself. The queen came into the room, and not observing that the baby was on the bed, opened another window. A frolicsome fairy wind, which had been watching for a chance of mischief, rushed in at the one window, and taking its way over the bed where the child was lying, caught her up, and rolling and floating her along like a piece of flue, or a dandelion seed, carried her with it through the opposite window, and away. The queen went downstairs, quite ignorant of the loss she had herself occasioned.

When the nurse returned, she supposed that her Majesty had carried her off, and, dreading a scolding, delayed making inquiry about her. But hearing nothing, she grew uneasy, and went at length to the queen's boudoir, where she found her Majesty.

"Please, your Majesty, shall I take the baby?" said she.

"Where is she?" asked the queen.

"Please forgive me. I know it was wrong."

"What do you mean?" said the queen, looking grave.

"Oh! don't frighten me, your Majesty!" exclaimed the nurse, clasping her hands.

The queen saw that something was amiss, and fell down in a faint. The nurse rushed about the palace, screaming, "My baby! My baby!"

Every one ran to the queen's room. But the queen could give no orders. They soon found out, however, that the princess was missing, and in a moment the palace was like a beehive in a garden; and in one minute more the queen was brought to herself by a great shout and a clapping of hands. They had found the princess fast asleep under a rose-bush, to which the elvish little wind-puff had carried her, finishing its mischief by shaking a shower of red rose-leaves all over the little white sleeper. Startled by the noise the servants made, she woke, and, furious with glee, scattered the rose-leaves in all directions, like a shower of spray in the sunset.

She was watched more carefully after this, no doubt; yet it would be endless to relate all the odd incidents resulting from this peculiarity of the young princess. But there never was a baby in a house, not to say a palace, that kept the household in such constant good humour, at least below-stairs. If it was not easy for her nurses to hold her, at least she made neither their arms nor their hearts ache. And she was so nice to play at ball with! There was positively no danger of letting her fall. They might throw her down, or knock her down, or push her down, but couldn't let her down. It is true, they might let her fly into the fire or the coal-hole, or through the window; but none of these accidents had happened as yet. If you heard peals of laughter resounding from some unknown region, you might be sure enough of the cause. Going down into the kitchen, or the room, you would find Jane and Thomas, and Robert and Susan, all and sum, playing at ball with the little princess.

One step, two step...

Bumps-a-daisy! Baby's first step is an equally momentous moment for mother. If she is lucky, she will be there to see it and catch baby in her arms! For a while now baby has been crawling swiftly about the place, discovering that things can be grasped with sticky fingers and held firmly. At a certain point, baby will struggle up into a standing position, holding on for dear life to a chair, table leg, or whatever feels safest. This is the moment of truth: "Mmm—the world looks so much better from up here!"

Then comes standing up alone, which is quite a wobbly affair at first. Usually, baby plants two little palms firmly on the floor and lifts up the hindquarters. There is a moment of hesitation before daring to trust the feet for balancing on. Then the body is carefully raised and another moment of contemplation follows before gravity demands forward motion—and the first step is taken!

Quite often this ends in a rather undignified fashion with a bump on the behind. Baby immediately looks around for an audience, and if there is one available, makes the most of it with a display of vocal crying, amply rewarded by mother's proud sympathy. However, if nobody's around, baby promptly tries to stand up again right away and get on with the big experiment. Finally, one step turns into two, and three and four and five and…Bingo! Mother! What a star!

And she agrees! But actually, there is no real correlation between brilliance and this early "milestone" achievement. From about nine months on, each baby chooses a personal moment to walk. Bare feet are best for this—"baby walkers" have been thoroughly discredited.

Florence Cheele

I'm From...

I'm from bath times in the kitchen sink,

From Johnson's soap and Mom's perfume;

I'm from sunflowers by the fence (golden

    yellow, dusty-faced, they beamed at me).

I'm from the ivy scrambling up the apple tree

    whose sturdy trunk grew from the ground

Like my solid, planted, feet.

KATE ASHTON

Bath time fun

Baby's bath time is a misnomer. For a start, it implies that baby bathes, which implies that it's just baby getting wet. In fact, it's mother who gets wet…she and anyone else in the near or far vicinity. It is true that baby might actually get bathed, but if this occurs it will be more by default than any other factor. Indeed, it's hard to imagine how the sort of anarchy that prevails at baby's bath time is even allowed in any self-respecting, decent household.

For a start, there's the timing—a matter for wide debate among the members of the care team because everybody wants to join in the fun. It's the loveliest thing in the world, baby's bath time. And then there's the location. Bathroom? Not enough space. Tub in baby's bedroom? Baby's too old for that. Kitchen sink? Baby's too big to lie down in it, the faucets get in the way, and so do basic rules of hygiene.

So a bathtub full of water is run to just the right temperature. Mild soap and a soft towel are at hand. Baby, sweetly naked but kicking and squalling, is lowered gently into the water. Wonder of wonders! Silence! Pure, unadulterated silence and a look upon the tiny face of rather surprised pleasure. Splash. Splash, splash. This is nice. Very nice and very funny. Splash, splash, SPLASH!!!

People begin to leave the scene, despite the fun. Soon mother will be quite alone. There is not enough space in the bathroom. There could never have been enough space. Not even artist David Hockney's biggest and bluest swimming pool could have accommodated such a surfeit of fun. How does baby manage to splash like that? The little cutie's not that big. And can't possibly be that strong. Surely not. And you can't get near the wriggling body to do a thing about it.

Baby's gloriously in charge and you're wet. Very wet. The floor is now under a good inch of water. And all the dear little ducks, boats, balls, and bits and bobs that dive and float, make letters, and blow bubbles, are also outside the bathtub and making their way slowly and inexorably toward a safe harbor behind the toilet or the sink. Some will soon pass through the bathroom door and sail in solemn procession down the stairs and into every other room in the house.

It's high time baby was got out of there, and by now, of course, you're quite prepared to overlook the question of whether or not the infant body has all been washed. Soap no longer comes into the equation, if it ever did. It's just you or junior. Meanwhile, there's very little water left in the bathtub so it should be a simple matter of reaching in and lifting baby out. If only everything wasn't so slippery. Ah, gotcha... wriggle, kick, deadly stare (how dare you spoil my fun?), squall... Hey, isn't this where we came in?

Toothy, toothy tiger

Some of the most beautiful objects given to baby at birth can be decorative teething rings. Many mothers treasure these forever, along with baby's shed baby-teeth. Some rings made of precious materials such as silver, ivory, or amber, become family heirlooms. Silver rattles used to serve the double function of entertaining and soothing baby, the cool, silky metal being very comforting when pressed against those inflamed little gums.

At about six months, increased salivation or drooling, irritability, loss of appetite, a rash or red discoloration appearing on the cheeks, restlessness or ear-pulling may herald the eruption of the first baby teeth. Twenty are due, so this can make for quite a period of misery.

The best remedies are cooled (not frozen) teething rings; a cold, wet cloth to suck on; and soft foods. Massaging the gums gently with the finger also helps, and in Scotland, the finger is sometimes moistened with just a touch of whiskey, the "water of life"—a wonderful analgesic! Chewing on sweet or frozen things, though, is absolutely not recommended for the little ones.

For generations, American mothers have given their teething babies the eminently graspable and nutritious bagel. In 1683, a Jewish baker in Vienna first made these boiled and baked stirrup-shaped yeast dough rings for the king of Poland, an enthusiastic horseman. He wanted to thank the king for saving some of his countrymen from Turkish invaders, and named the rings "bagels"—*bugel* being German for "riding stirrup." Bagels became popular in Poland, where they gained sanction as presents for women in childbirth, even getting a mention in community registers. And mothers, being the innovative people that they have always been, soon passed bagels into their portfolio of remedies.

Time for bed

Some children just will not go to bed. Mother reads sleep-inducing stories, talks quietly, takes the child on her knee, cajoles, argues, discusses the matter, and finally insists. But no go. At last, tested beyond endurance, she threatens punishments or gives up and simply curls up in bed beside her recalcitrant offspring. Sure enough, the next thing she knows, she has slept there half the night; she has a bad dose of bunk-bed cramp, is completely exhausted, and faces a repeat performance when evening comes.

In fact, all young children go through the developmental phase of "separation anxiety" and bedtime is exactly that—a time of separation. So in a way, it is quite natural for them to try to postpone it: the sheer variety of devices devised for this purpose is a cause for wonder. One child was found more than an hour after she had been sent to bed, sitting quietly at the bottom of the stairs reading all that was available at this location: the telephone directory.

After infancy a child should no longer need rocking or feeding before sleep and a quiet, firm ritual will serve to establish habits of going to bed alone. Luckily, children usually get over all their sleep disturbances as they mature. The effect on adults, however, is cumulative, so mothers have every reason to look after their own interests at bedtime.

Do you want the stars to play with?
Or the moon to run away with—
They'll come if you don't cry.

TRADITIONAL

All Through the Night

Sleep, my babe, lie still and slumber,
All through the night;
Guardian angels God will lend thee,
All through the night;
Soft and drowsy hours are creeping,
Hill and vale in slumber sleeping,
Mother dear her watch is keeping,
All through the night.

God is here, thou'lt not be lonely,
All through the night;
'Tis not I who guards thee only,
All through the night.
Night's dark shades will soon be over,
Still my watchful care shall hover,
God with me His watch is keeping,
All through the night.

CRADLE SONG

'Tis time for all children on earth
To think about getting to bed!

NURSERY RHYME

Hopi Lullaby

Sleep, sleep, sleep.
In the trail, the beetles
On each other's backs are sleeping,
So on mine, my baby, you.
Sleep, sleep, sleep.

Golden Slumbers

Golden slumbers kiss your eyes,
Smiles awake you when you rise.
Sleep, pretty wantons; do not cry,
And I will sing a lullaby:
Rock them, rock them, lullaby.

Care is heavy, therefore sleep you;
You are care, and care must keep you.
Sleep, pretty wantons; do not cry,
And I will sing a lullaby:
Rock them, rock them, lullaby.

THOMAS DEKKER

Hush Little Baby

Hush little baby
don't say a word,
Mama's gonna buy you
a mocking bird,

If that mocking bird don't sing,
Mama's gonna buy you
a diamond ring,

If that diamond ring gets broke,
Mama's gonna buy you
a billy goat,

If that billy goat don't pull,
Mama's gonna buy you
a cart 'n bull,

If that cart 'n bull turn over,
Mama's gonna buy you
a dog named Rover,

If that dog named Rover
don't bark,
Mama's gonna buy you
a horse 'n cart,

Hush little baby don't say
a word,
Mama's gonna buy you
a mocking bird,

If that mocking bird don't sing,
Mama's gonna buy you
a diamond ring,

If that diamond ring don't shine,
Hush little baby don't you mind,

Cuz if that diamond ring
don't shine,
Mama's gonna love you
'til the end of time.

*There never was a child
so lovely but his mother
was glad to get him asleep.*

RALPH WALDO EMERSON

Please, give me sleep!

Sleeping problems are a common complication of child-rearing. And they involve both parents and child. If this were explained to unsuspecting parents-to-be at the outset, there might be fewer complaints. As it is, parents on every part of the globe discover the horrors of sleep deprivation too late to do anything about it. Because we all know that babies can't be sent back.

So, with the joys of parenthood begin the lesser joys of waiting for moments of peace, perfect peace. These can seem very few and far between. Meanwhile, demands remain at the same level of exorbitance, and something of an imbalance is created. Some fathers fall asleep on their unknown neighbor's shoulder on the bus or subway in the morning. This is treated with brusque solidarity or as an outright imposition, depending on the neighbor's own stage of parenting. Mothers awaken in a numb daze at five in the morning. After all, two feedings a night are acceptable. But breast-feeding babies may easily want seven!

At age two, children try to control the environment and demand a say in when and how they go to bed. A little leeway helps here, but overall control has to remain with the parent. A child of under three may wake at night simply from not being sure whether mommy and daddy will be there while he or she sleeps. The toddler has to wake up to check. Soothing comfort is what's needed and/or a temporary mattress near to mother and father. A much-loved old blanket or toy to cuddle can help. But the middle of the night is not a time for full-fledged games.

Children need a routine to establish good bedtime habits. Cozy, intimate rituals of talking and reading at the bedside make for comforting associations with this time of day. Bottles of any sort, or muddles of toys, have no place in the crib; this needs to be a restful place rather than an amusement park. Bed should never be used as a threat, so sending a child to bed, with or without a full tummy, is never a good idea. After they start school, children need nine to twelve hours' sleep a night, and this is when sleep deprivation can start to become bad news. Too much television and caffeinated drinks seem to be the main culprits.

All around the world and all around the clock, parents are trying to get their children to sleep, using whatever tactics seem appropriate. One of the most reliable methods is simply rocking the baby. Another is holding the baby close to mother's body while she walks around. Another is singing a lullaby. Another is sleeping at the breast. Some people take their children into bed with them; some absolutely won't. But all new parents learn to survive on far less sleep than they feel they deserve. And crying about it is only for babies.

A mother's arms are made of tenderness and children sleep soundly in them.

VICTOR HUGO

Oh those baby blues!

Nothing can prepare a brand-new mother for such an unexpected, confusing, and upsetting experience as postnatal depression (PND). It brings sadness at the happiest moment in her life and a strenuous lesson in nurturing symbiotic souls, her baby's and her own.

However, baby blues are surprisingly commonplace. In fact, 50 to 80 percent of mothers experience a mild form of depression after the birth of their babies. This lasts only a few hours or days and has several possible causes. Hormone levels are in flux at this time and might trigger the blues. Weariness after the birth could be another cause. Most mothers are completely unprepared for this degree of tiredness, created by apprehension before the birth, physical exhaustion, emotional relief, and release afterward. Indeed the period before and during the birth can be a roller coaster.

And although rest and quiet are recommended after giving birth, in real life those commodities are suddenly in very short supply. There is a new baby to care for and feed. Visitors come and sometimes stay too long. Sleep is disrupted. Mother or baby may have some small health problem that causes worry out of all proportion, or there may be feeding difficulties. Then there are the normal anxieties of any new mother about being left alone with her baby for the first time: she worries about how she will cope and what to do in unfamiliar situations.

So the last things she needs when she's feeling blue are cheery admonitions that everything will be fine! It is much more helpful to be able to talk to someone qualified to give sound advice: a health visitor, midwife, or doctor. Loving and understanding words from her partner or another family member also go a long way, or even just the feeling that there is someone on the end of the phone line who will listen. Mostly, baby blues subside naturally. But lasting symptoms—sleeplessness, sadness, anxiety, panic attacks, fear, sex aversion, lethargy, and exhaustion—indicate a case of true postnatal depression and ask to be taken more seriously.

The best thing is to talk to a doctor. Sometimes counseling or analysis can help. Sometimes drugs will be prescribed. But the main thing is that the mother's illness is acknowledged. Being reminded how lucky she is and what a beautiful baby she's got are just about the last thing she needs. Already, it's very hard for her to think about being nice to herself. She needs care. And of course, in the end this will be best for baby too.

Expert help and support, medical treatment, and the love and care of family are vital to counter PND, as is the understanding of a partner who is also facing a new and sometimes frightening situation and may feel hurt and rejected. The more love, affection, and sympathetic ears the new mother finds, the sooner she will begin to recover, although it may take weeks or months. And, unfortunately, subsequent pregnancies could bring the same problem. So psychological preparation is advisable for mother, partner, and family too.

Anne of Green Gables

by

LUCY MAUD MONTGOMERY

When Marilla took Anne up to bed that night she said stiffly: "Now, Anne, I noticed last night that you threw your clothes all about the floor when you took them off. That is a very untidy habit, and I can't allow it at all. As soon as you take off any article of clothing fold it neatly and place it on the chair. I haven't any use at all for little girls who aren't neat."

"I was so harrowed up in my mind last night that I didn't think about my clothes at all," said Anne. "I'll fold them nicely tonight. They always made us do that at the asylum. Half the time, though, I'd forget, I'd be in such a hurry to get into bed nice and quiet and imagine things."

"You'll have to remember a little better if you stay here," admonished Marilla. "There, that looks something like. Say your prayers now and get into bed."

"I never say any prayers," announced Anne.

Marilla looked with horrified astonishment.

"Why, Anne, what do you mean? Were you never taught to say your prayers? God always wants little girls to say their prayers. Don't you know who God is, Anne?"

"God is a spirit, infinite, eternal and unchangeable, in His being, wisdom, power, holiness, justice, goodness, and truth," responded Anne promptly and glibly.

Marilla looked rather relieved.

"So you do know something then, thank goodness! You're not quite a heathen. Where did you learn that?"

"Oh, at the asylum Sunday-school. They made us learn the whole catechism. I liked it pretty well. There's something splendid about some of the words. 'Infinite, eternal and unchangeable.' Isn't that grand? It has such a roll to it—just like a big organ playing. You couldn't quite call it poetry, I suppose, but it sounds a lot like it, doesn't it?"

"We're not talking about poetry, Anne—we are talking about saying your prayers. Don't you know it's a terrible wicked thing not to say your prayers every night? I'm afraid you are a very bad little girl."

"You'd find it easier to be bad than good if you had red hair," said Anne reproachfully. "People who haven't red hair don't know what trouble is. Mrs. Thomas told me that God made my hair red ON PURPOSE, and I've never cared about Him since. And anyhow I'd always be too tired at night to bother saying prayers. People who have to look after twins can't be expected to say their prayers. Now, do you honestly think they can?"

Marilla decided that Anne's religious training must be begun at once. Plainly there was no time to be lost. "You must say your prayers while you are under my roof, Anne."

"Why, of course, if you want me to," assented Anne cheerfully.

"I'd do anything to oblige you. But you'll have to ☞

tell me what to say for this once. After I get into bed I'll imagine out a real nice prayer to say always. I believe that it will be quite interesting, now that I come to think of it."

"You must kneel down," said Marilla in embarrassment.

Anne knelt at Marilla's knee and looked up gravely.

"Why must people kneel down to pray? If I really wanted to pray I'll tell you what I'd do. I'd go out into a great big field all alone or into the deep, deep, woods, and I'd look up into the sky—up—up—up—into that lovely blue sky that looks as if there was no end to its blueness. And then I'd just FEEL a prayer. Well, I'm ready. What am I to say?"

Marilla felt more embarrassed than ever. She had intended to teach Anne the childish classic, "Now I lay me down to sleep." But she had, as I have told you, the glimmerings of a sense of humor—which is simply another name for a sense of fitness of things; and it suddenly occurred to her that that simple little prayer, sacred to white-robed childhood lisping at motherly knees, was entirely unsuited to this freckled witch of a girl who knew and cared nothing bout God's love, since she had never had it translated to her through the medium of human love.

"You're old enough to pray for yourself, Anne," she said finally. "Just thank God for your blessings and ask Him humbly for the things you want."

"Well, I'll do my best," promised Anne, burying her face in Marilla's lap. "Gracious heavenly Father—that's the way the ministers say it in church, so I suppose it's all right in private prayer, isn't it?" she interjected, lifting her head for a moment.

"Gracious heavenly Father, I thank Thee for the White Way of Delight and the Lake of Shining Waters and Bonny and the Snow Queen. I'm really extremely grateful for them. And that's all the blessings I can think of just now to thank Thee for. As for the things I want, they're so numerous that it would take a great deal of time to name them all so I will only mention the two most important. Please let me stay at Green Gables; and please let me be good-looking when I grow up. I remain, yours respectfully, Anne Shirley."

"There, did I do all right?" she asked eagerly, getting up. "I could have made it much more flowery if I'd had a little more time to think it over."

Poor Marilla was only preserved from complete collapse by remembering that it was not irreverence, but simply spiritual ignorance on the part of Anne that was responsible for this extraordinary petition. She tucked the child up in bed, mentally vowing that she should be taught a prayer the very next day, and was leaving the room with the light when Anne called her back.

"I've just thought of it now. I should have said, 'Amen' in place of 'yours respectfully,' shouldn't I?—the way the ministers do. I'd forgotten it, but I felt a prayer should be finished off in some way, so I put in the other. Do you suppose it will make any difference?"

"I—don't suppose it will," said Marilla. "Go to sleep now like a good child. Good night."

I remember my mother's prayers and they have always followed me. They have clung to me all my life.

ABRAHAM LINCOLN

The Great Mother

One fine day a child will ask the little question, "What is God?" Mother might as well be prepared for this, otherwise she might find herself trying to hide under the ironing or just plain bluffing. And that would be a terrible cop-out, because the truth is, mother is the sacred source of all life in mythology.

According to ancient Indo-European sacred beliefs, the female antedates and includes the male, and mortal woman embodies these principles. The Chinese Tao, or Way of Heaven, dating back to 1500 B.C., accepts the same concept, saying: "He that knoweth his Mother, (Tao) and abideth in Her nature, remaineth in surety all his days." Tantric "threads," or teachings, from even earlier times speak of Tara, the preVedic Savior Goddess known from India to Ireland as ruler of the Underworld, Earth, and Heavens; birth, death, regeneration, love, war, the seasons, all that lives and grows, and the moon cycles—every aspect of life, in fact.

In ancient Athens, a festival nicknamed "The Rioting" for its wild, orgiastic customs celebrated Taramata, or Mother Tara. Perhaps Tara became Gaia, the great Earth Mother who gave birth to Uranus—the sky—and rain, plants, animals, and monsters such as the one-eyed Cyclops. Uranus banished these to the Underworld, and Gaia, heartbroken at his cruelty, gave birth to the Tritons, ancestors of a new generation of gods. Under the leadership of Kronos, the Tritons attacked their father with a scythe, taking away his power.

Kronos married his sister Rhea and had six children, but hearing that one would kill him, Kronos swallowed five of them; the sixth, Zeus, was saved by his mother from this fate and spent his childhood amongst the nymphs. When he grew up, Zeus gave his father a potion so that he coughed up the other five children. Among these were Ceres or Demeter, goddess of the earth, fertility, corn, and agriculture; Pluto, ruler of the Underworld; and Poseidon, ruler of the Oceans.

Pluto abducted Demeter's daughter Persephone, taking her to the Underworld. Persephone might have remained there forever, but Demeter negotiated a custody agreement with her wicked brother and after that, Persephone was allowed to spend half her time on the earth. But maternal grief during the six months of the year that her daughter lived in the Underworld made Demeter vow that during that period, nothing should flourish upon earth. And that is how the seasons began.

The central idea of the maternal or creative principle has become enshrined in all religions. In Judaism, the religion passes down through the female line. Both Islam and Christianity honor the sacred nature of Mary, mother of Jesus Christ, whose birth is recorded in the Koran and in the Bible. All sacred writings recognize and celebrate the universal mystery and wonder of birth. It forms the very basis of our spiritual search, the one that begins as a child with the little question, "What is God?"

God hail thee, Mary, full of grace, the Lord is with thee; blessed art thou among women, and blessed is the Fruit of thy womb, Jesus.

The godmother

At the birth or baptism of her child, a mother will often appoint a good friend as godmother. Many a new godmother receives this request with a strange combination of pride and confusion. What is expected of her? Everyone has heard of the fairy godmother and is flattered to be thought capable of her kind deeds, such as turning Cinderella into a princess for the evening, for example, and pumpkins into carriages. But godmother without the prefix—what does that entail?

The custom of appointing godparents for children dates back to early Christian times. Believers were then being widely persecuted and life was altogether less predictable than it is today. The idea was that, in the absence of the parents, a child would have someone to offer solace, shelter, and—most importantly—spiritual guidance. In the Roman Catholic Church, godparents are called "sponsors," underlining their role in support of the faith.

The godmother traditionally gives her godchild a baptismal gift symbolizing this relationship: a Bible, a crucifix, or a special book. She is supposed to remember significant dates in the life of her godchild, but it is vital that she prays for the child and is always there for him or her.

One spinster lady had 26 godchildren. She kept a chart of all their birthdays, baptisms, favorite things, and landmarks in their lives, updating them every day. The chart hung at the foot of her bed, the first thing she saw in the morning and the last at night. One godchild reported that in a long and difficult life, her greatest source of strength had been the knowledge that her godmother was praying for her each day. So perhaps for some, the power of prayer is even greater than a fairy spell.

THE CHILD'S QUEST

My mother twines me roses wet with dew;
Oft have I sought the garden through and through;
I cannot find the tree whereon
My mother's roses grew.
Seek not, O child, the tree whereon
Thy mother's roses grew.

My mother tells me tales of noble deeds;
Oft have I sought her book when no one heeds;
I cannot find the page, alas,
From which my mother reads.
Seek not, O child, to find the page
From which thy mother reads.

My mother croons me songs all soft and low,
Through the white night where little breezes blow;
Yet never when the morning dawns,
My mother's songs I know.
Seek not, O child, at dawn of day
Thy mother's songs to know.

FRANCES SHAW

How does it grow?

Watching things grow, a mother and child together discover the wonders of nature. The miracle of a growing seedling demonstrates to a child both the pleasure and the great importance of plants, for you can eat them too! A packet of mustard seeds is the best beginning. Sprinkle these on damp cotton wool in a shallow container; place on a sunny windowsill, water every couple of days, and a week later shoots will appear that you can cut and use in salads.

You can have extra fun by turning a yogurt container into a funny face with the mustard sprouts growing out of the top like green fluffy hair. Just wash the container and paint it white, put a face on it, and plant the seeds on a thin layer of cotton wool on top of moistened, crumpled-up paper towels, leaving about an inch (2.5cm) clear at the top of the pot. Or you can grow little green-haired people (see pages 92–95).

Fun Project: 1
Eggheads

You will need

- Clean eggshells, tops taken off
- Fabric, wool, scraps of colored paper
- Cardboard tube (from toilet roll)
- Popsicle sticks, one for each egg
- Cotton wool

- Mustard seeds
- Sequins, stickers, buttons
- Paints, paintbrushes
- Felt-tip pens
- Scissors, glue

Making the sprouting eggheads:

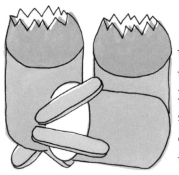

1 Cut a popsicle stick in half, crosswise, and glue the two pieces to the bottom of the cardboard tube, to make an X-shaped support for it. Use stickers, buttons, and fabric to decorate the tube body. Paint the popsicle stick "feet."

92

2 Balance an eggshell on the top of the tube and paint or draw a face on the egg.

3 Carefully fill the shell with water and cotton wool. Sprinkle with mustard seeds, then put the egghead in a dark place.

4 When the green shoots appear, move the egghead to a bright place. Sprinkle water on the cotton wool every day.

Make a mustache and eyebrows from short fringes of wool and glue a fabric tie onto a paper shirt.

Stick on round stickers for eyes and a pair of gold curtain rings or washers for earrings.

94

This puppy has balloon ears and a wool tail!

When the leaves appear, snip the cress for your sandwich—Yummy!

When I am grown to man's estate
I shall be very proud and great
And tell the other girls and boys,
Not to meddle with my toys.

ROBERT LOUIS STEVENSON

One, two, buckle my shoe,
Three, four, knock at the door.

NURSERY RHYME

I can dress myself

One fine morning, a child will suddenly announce that he or she can get dressed alone. But there are just ten minutes before it is time to leave, so mother has a dilemma. She knows that, for her child, dressing involves complicated decision-making, discussion, prioritizing, and philosophizing.

Help! What to do? The desperate mother, eye on the clock, simply refuses to enter into any form of negotiation and just tries to get on with the job. But then she runs straight into that magic form of passive resistance in which her child disappears into a dream world far removed from the present. This means hoisting limp little limbs in and out of sleeves, pants-legs, and jackets, discovering on the way that everything has suddenly and mysteriously shrunk or turned itself inside out.

Saintly mothers take time to patiently explain the procedure as they go along and resist the temptation to do everything for junior until the mysterious skills are mastered. Others just throw up their hands and leave it entirely to the child! One three-year-old thus left the house in her favorite ensemble: a glittery fairy dress worn over striped pants, accented by bright red plastic boots. Her mother found an innovative way to cope: "I just put a sticker on her front saying 'I dressed myself today!' As she pointed out, "That way, she gets a sense of pride and I'm not to blame for letting her go around looking so weird!"

"Of course you know your
A B C?" said the Red Queen.
"To be sure I do."

LEWIS CARROLL

Sweet infant, innocently gay,
With blooming face arrayed in peaceful smiles,
How light thy cheerful heart doth sportive play,
Unconscious of all future cares and toils.

ANON

You're a big person now!

A child's first day at school can be a bittersweet moment for mother! She'll never forget that parting, full of anguish and pride. When the big day arrives she hardly knows whether it is she or her child who has most needed all that careful preparation—the exciting stories she's told about school, and the walks past the gates to watch the other children coming out at the end of the afternoon. Dressed in new things, gripping her schoolbag eagerly, the child looks up to say goodbye, ready to march happily into the classroom. But, oh no! It is mother who can't stop the tears brimming! Meanwhile, she sees other mothers on their knees, trying to persuade adamant "refuseniks" that school's truly a fine place!

One little girl, triumphant at having survived her first day, thought she had cracked this school business once and for all. And so she was outraged to learn that she had to go there again the next day, and the next, and the next... "'That's why they're called lessons,' said the Gryphon, 'because they lessen and lessen.'" Yes, Lewis Carroll knew all about it.

And so did the "Father of American Education," Horace Mann, who advocated universal, free, nonsectarian public school. He declared, "As an apple is not in any sense an apple until it is ripe, so a human being is not in any proper sense a human being until he is educated." That's all very well, but it is also a hard lesson for a mother to learn that from now on, instead being her child's whole world, she is now the safe harbor to which the child returns.

Bigger and better every day

"Do you know who made you?" "Nobody as I knowed on,"
said the child, with a short laugh... "I 'spect I growed."

HARRIET BEECHER STOWE

Making a chart to record how tall the children are growing is lots of
fun. The growth chart may be the result of an afternoon's creative play,
with mother and children drawing the chart on a zany, decorative
background—giant flowers or vegetables are favorites because they
have nice tall stalks and bold colors. Alternatively, a simple vertical
measure on the bedroom wall or door will suffice. Either way,
comparing growth rates can encourage harmless competition
between children. They all like to know the rate at which they're
getting taller—it gives them a sense of measurable progress in life.

Mothers enjoy watching children revel in their growth also—
especially as it's one of the best indicators of good health and
well-being. Inevitably, any mother's self-confidence is boosted
simultaneously with her child's pride. So how does she assess growth
progress? Normal heights are difficult to define, but some basic rules
apply: for instance, the child of tall parents is likely to grow up to be
tall, and so on. As a useful guideline, at four years, a child should have
doubled his or her birth height; and by thirteen years, he or she
should have tripled it. In between, you may reckon that the age of the
child, multiplied by two and a half times, plus 30 inches (12cm), gives
the average height.

105

Togetherness

Playing, reading, watching television, games, eating—whatever it is, doing it together with mother makes it special. Togetherness is the ingredient that turns any activity into an "experience," because as soon as there are two of you, there are surprises, laughter, sharing and daring, and double the fun. As soon as the imagination is let loose in play, it longs for someone else's to bounce off. And mother is the perfect partner.

Doing things together allows mother to expand her child's inborn creativity. All she has to do is admire everything: a drawing or painting, a wobbly building-brick tower, a little fat modelling clay worm. And of course, everything has a story attached to it. The tower is inhabited by two princesses, their grandmother, and a wicked witch; the worm lived under the ground until he came up for air and was captured by a giant ...

And the stories all lead to games, because the tower needs a castle and the castle needs a hill and the hill needs sheep and the sheep need a farm. And then the princesses have to escape, but the wicked witch won't let them. And so the big, strong, good giant steps over the world to come and rescue them; but they've been thrown into a dark dungeon and so he can't find them—Until his magic worm starts to glow...

And the games lead to explanations. For can worms really

glow? And what is a witch? And what is a princess, too, actually? Lengthy discussions follow, during which the world is described and everything put in its proper place, more or less, and things begin to make some kind of sense. Because it's the most enormous, mystifying mystery at first—to all of us.

The explanations lead on to demonstrations, which lead to role-playing. The child can play mothers with mother, fathers with father, driving, washing, cooking, and going off to work. The real-life stuff has to be improved upon and we get fantasy. Make-believe becomes a play in which everyone has his or her own special role. The play gets performed. The applause is addictive. And so another play is written, and then a tiny poem. An artist is born!

Reading with mother becomes reading alone, but it's still so lovely to be able to discuss the story with her. There are so many wrong bits, so many little places where it didn't quite make sense. And it's so awful when the story ends and you feel so lonely and wonder where all the characters have gone and what they did next and no, mother absolutely wont let you choose another book yet. Not alone, anyway.

And reading alternates with watching television together. Watching television with mother makes it better because you can ask questions and she turns it off just when you are getting really tired. And then you have supper together because father's not home yet, and that's so cozy, and then she gets you ready for bed and there's that huge cuddle before you go to sleep …

Food, glorious food!

There is plenty of good advice about food around for mothers. It goes something like this: "Lots of it." "A mother's attitude towards food will rub off on her children." "What she has in the house, they'll (have to) eat." "Start off right and the rest will follow." The platitudes are many, but the reality boils down to one thing: kids love junk food. They prefer it to everything else and the manufacturers know that, nurture the desire, and get rich quick while mothers get the blame.

So when she tries to turn the tide single-handedly, she finds herself like King Canute, sitting on the edge of an ever-encroaching sea with her shoes still on. Trying to introduce whole-wheat bread, for example, is tantamount to serving plain old straw. Organic foods "don't taste of anything." Fruit in the lunchbox is ultimately uncool. Anything "polyunsaturated" belongs in the laundry or the science lab—they don't mind which, just as long as it doesn't land up on their plate.

But children have one weakness: they are all the most outrageous snobs. They'll buy into anything sassy, smooth, sophisticated, or endorsed by celebrity chefs. So the smart mother simply exploits this situation by naming and faming food. Every kind of exotic title can be dreamed up to enhance the eat-me appeal. Finely-cut carrot and celery sticks can become "batons" and that yogurt and chili dip "Bohemian rhapsody"!

Turkey ham rolls stuffed with cottage cheese and baked with a light tomato sauce becomes "poulet provençale"... you get the rough idea. And then the gorgeous garnish! Even healthy food can be made to look fabulous. Especially healthy food can be made to look fabulous. In the end, aesthetics do matter. Nothing looks sadder, heavier-hearted, or more sorry for itself than a lonely little organic brown bread roll. Even if it does fill you up and keep you slim.

The equally sad lunchbox has to be turned into a cool accessory by mixing retro and new ideas. A bag of potato chips is fine, now and then. Ditto for cookies. And candy. But the balance can be shifted in favor of new flavors. Fat-free sandwich fillings can be spiced up with chopped nuts or herbs. Put in an exotic fruit or two or a hunk of cucumber to chew on.

Fruit bars and natural fruit drinks are coming back into fashion, and a good thing too. A smart container eases the phasing-out of fizzy drinks, to be replaced by mineral water, and several tiny packs of different juices are more fun than one big one that gets warm and stale as the school day wears on.

And any positive change in home diet will surely influence the children. It might take a few years, but it'll work in the end. Good basic ingredients are key. The better and healthier these are, the more they can be eaten raw. And no matter who does the cooking,, the meal will still be a whole lot better for everyone than any junk food alternative.

Ma's magic chicken noodle soup with vegetables

Serve them this warming, nourishing soup—your children will feel loved and secure forever.

Serves 6

8 cups/2 liters chicken stock (preferably homemade)

1 large onion, finely chopped

3 carrots, halved lengthwise and thinly sliced

2 celery stalks, thinly sliced

2 small zucchini (courgettes), thinly sliced (optional)

4oz/120g thin egg noodles (vermicelli) or other pasta

1 cup/200g shredded or diced cooked chicken

2 tbsp/15ml finely chopped parsley

Salt and freshly ground black pepper

Saltine crackers, soup crackers, or water biscuits, to serve (optional)

1 Pour the chicken stock into a pot and bring to the boil over a medium-high heat. Skim off any fat or foam that rises to the surface. Reduce the heat to medium.

2 Add the onion, carrots, and celery, and simmer for about 10 minutes, until the vegetables are just tender. Stir in the zucchini and cook for a further 3 minutes.

3 Add the noodles to the simmering soup and cook for 3–4 minutes or according to the directions on the package.

4 When the noodles are tender, stir in the cooked chicken and parsley, season with salt and pepper, and heat through. Serve steaming hot with crackers or water biscuits (if using).

Cook's tip
Cooking the noodles in the soup thickens the broth slightly. If you prefer a clear thin broth, cook the noodles separately, drain and rinse them before adding to the soup with the cooked chicken and parsley.

One can say everything best over a meal.

GEORGE ELIOT

Mother's trying to talk!

"Motherhood," sighed one (otherwise) devoted mother, "is just one long interrupted conversation." The Victorian era saw the rearing of children as one long exercise in discipline, distilled in the famous phrase, "Children should be seen and not heard." The sign of a good parent was one whose child was well behaved, and this meant mannerly, polite, respectful, and quiet. Children were taught to behave like small adults, to "respect their elders and betters," and to "know their place." But a more permissive mood dawned in the twentieth century, with new child psychologists such as Dr Benjamin Spock and Donald Winnicott telling us that the child has a right to talk too.

And of course they are right. But what about the well-behaved mother? You get up at the crack of dawn, do the laundry, clean up after breakfast, get the big ones off to school, the little one dressed, the baby into the stroller, and finally you're out in the fresh air with the front door mercifully closed behind you. And hey, just along the street, you meet an old friend whom you haven't seen for ages. So you get talking…

Then, just as the conversation's getting really gripping, there's a frantic tug on your coat, and your toddler absolutely MUST go to the bathroom, or over to Johnny's to play, NOW… and, yes, it's imperative! Even though you're dying to know what happened next…

The Chatterbox

From morning till night it was Lucy's delight
To chatter and talk without stopping:
There was not a day but she rattled away,
Like water for ever a-dropping.
No matter at all if the subjects were small,
Or not worth the trouble of saying,
'Twas equal to her, she would talking prefer
To working, or reading, or playing.
You'll think now, perhaps, that there would have been gaps,
If she had not been wonderfully clever:
That her sense was so great, and so witty her pate,
It would be forthcoming for ever;
But that's quite absurd, for have you not heard
That much tongue and few brains are connected?
That they are supposed to think least who talk most,
And their wisdom is always suspected?
While Lucy was young, had she bridled her tongue,
With a little good sense and exertion,
Who knows, but she might now have been our delight,
Instead of our jest and aversion?

ANN TAYLOR

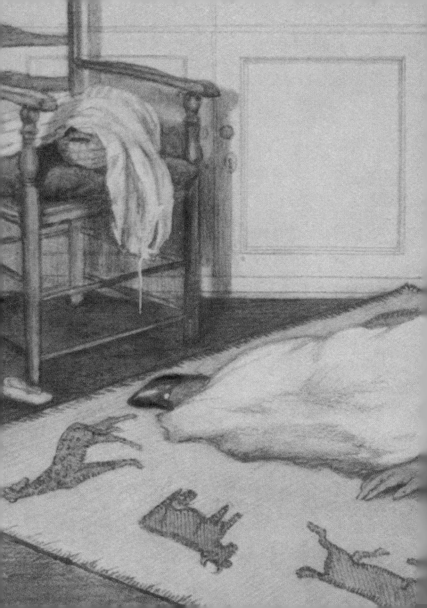

The mother's heart is
the child's schoolroom

HENRY WARD BEECHER

Swing high, swing low!

The playground offers great opportunities for mother to teach her children how to cope with important life situations. For example, just imagine what happens during a session on the swings. First you have to be lifted up off the ground and placed on that little, unsteady seat. And then mother pushes you off—away from her into the air. Eeek! Back you come, but instead of catching you and giving you a cuddle, she pushes you off again…Oooh!

Next there's the tough lesson about hanging on and not letting go. And not throwing up when you definitely want to. And trusting the world and elements you can't see. The wind goes whistling past your ears, the ground rushes away beneath and the sky makes you feel so small. The trees come up so close and everything down there is at such a funny angle.

Mmmm—but it's exciting! As long as mother doesn't go off somewhere and is there to get you down, you'll never again be afraid of abandonment to such an awesome, thrilling, airy fate—as long as she is there! She is. She lifts you to the ground and puts your lost shoe back on and gives you a huge hug and a big smile! See! You rode in the air, and were ever so clever and brave! But, strange to say, you have suddenly discovered how much you liked it. More than that, you want to go on again, now, please. And could she push you higher, higher, higher…STOP! That's high enough!

I can see the tops of the trees and over the wall and I don't feel sick at all. I'm not afraid, I'm like a bird, so free!

COME FLY MY KITE

Any mother who has ever stood on a windy beach or hill teaching her child how to fly a kite knows the sheer thrill of watching it soar into the air, the tug on the string, and the wonderful swooping sensation that travels down it. Letting your child hold the string for the first time and holding on to him so that both don't blow away is quite an experience.

The Chinese say that to fly a kite is to let your own soul take flight. This would certainly explain the exhilaration—and the despair when it crashes to the ground instead of landing decorously nearby. But better this than entanglement in a tree, or worse...

"Kity, Whity, Flighty, Kity, Out of sighty... little kite!" If Edward Lear knew not to give out too much line too soon, to let the kite rise slowly on the air's thermal currents, taking its own time to climb aloft; if he knew, why didn't we? Oh, agony!

Kites have a long and illustrious history. In the South Sea Islands, they have always been used to carry the bait when fishing. In the Polynesian islands, they were associated with the gods. The Maori people made kites in the shape of birds, *manu*, to carry messages to the gods, one of whom was even an ancestor of the kite. China is widely held to be the birthplace of the kite, and China and Japan used them for military purposes. The Koreans write the names of male children on kites; in Thailand each monarch had his own kite, and in Japan kites shaped like carps, which symbolize strength and fortitude, are flown on May 5, Children's Day.

Fun Project: 2
Flying fish kite

You will need

- Thick colored paper, about 1ft/30cm square
- Colored paper (large sheet)
- Paints or felt-tip pens
- Paintbrushes
- Stickers
- Cord or thick thread, about 30ft/10m
- 3 square stickers or pieces of sticky tape
- Hole-punch
- Scissors

Making a miniature kite

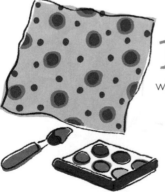

1 Decorate the square of thick paper on both sides with paint or felt-tip pen.

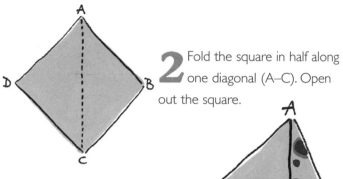

Fold the square in half along
one diagonal (A–C). Open
out the square.

2

Fold the side A–B to
meet the center fold.
Fold A–D to meet the center
fold in the same way. Flatten
the folds.

3

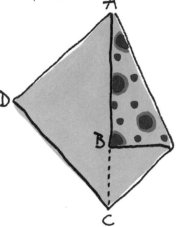

Stick a square sticker on the
tip of the kite, punch a hole
and tie 3 feet (1m) of cord
through it. Twist paper rectangles,
$1\frac{1}{4} \times 1\frac{1}{2}$ inches (3 × 6cm),
onto the tail.

4

5 Stick square stickers on the two corners, folded to the back. Punch a hole in each one. Loop cord through the holes and knot it, leaving the rest of the cord dangling.

6 Turn the kite over. On the front, paint a large eye and a fin in a contrasting color. Fly the Flying Fish kite by the long piece of cord tied at the back.

Twist rectangles of paper or crepe paper at intervals down the tail, adding a dot of glue to keep each one in place.

Decorate your flying fish kite with bright spots or squiggles of paint, and don't forget a big, watchful eye.

These kites are designed to be used in a light breeze—they will tear if you fly them in a gale-force wind!

The square stickers prevent the cord from tearing the paper.

Fun by the sea ...

When I was down beside the sea
A wooden spade they gave to me
To dig the sandy shore.

ROBERT LOUIS STEVENSON

The happiest vacations are spent beside the sea, where mother can lie in the sun while her child enjoys hours of play in the sand. Take only the simplest toys—bucket, spade, and ball being the most important. Everything else is kindly provided by nature.

As for other necessities, today's designer sun gear for mother and child includes maximum-protection sunscreen; beach umbrella; loose, soft clothing in natural fibers; and the absolutely de rigueur floppy hat—much cooler than a baseball cap! And then of course there are the funky sunglasses with sun filter you buy to replace those bright pink plastic ones some little person borrowed specially for the vacation from an accommodating best friend ...

Building sandcastles, collecting shells, and paddling in the sea are summer's endless gifts to us. Some people simply can't give it up, and go on to become adult sand sculptors, entering competitions and winning big prizes. The magic formula for building castles is one part water to eight parts sand, and some boffins have even applied themselves to finding the best beaches for it, researching load-bearing capacity, grain-size distribution, visual aesthetics, and cleanliness ... and you thought those boffins were all busy with rocket science, didn't you?

Seaside picnic

The whole charm of the seaside picnic lies in the sand—sand as in sandcastle and sand as in sandwich. And while father may take charge of the former occupation, it is mother who has to deal with the latter. She gets the worst bargain, as usual. Because sand is the whole fun and fundamental property of a sandcastle, whereas for a sandwich it is an extra, an unplanned ingredient added at the last moment as if by a stroke of nature's culinary genius. However perfect the picnic she has planned and prepared, she is powerless to prevent this less than divine intervention. Sand gets just about everywhere. And then somewhere.

Yet nothing makes people hungrier than playing on the beach and swimming in the sea. Back they run, laughing and shivering in equal measure and scattering sea all over the checked cloth laid out lovingly in the shade of the beach umbrella. Wrapped up in copious towels, they continue to laugh and shiver and bite the towels and make no effort to get dry. At last they sit down, still dripping, still in towels, still shivering, and demand to know what there is to eat.

Well, what is there to eat? The great secret of a seaside picnic is simplicity: as few niches for sand to get in as possible.

So go for chicken, roasted at home with fresh thyme and grated lemon zest butter pushed under its breast skin; the rest of the lemon halved in the cavity. Cool, cut up and transport in a coolbox. Take couscous in a big plastic bowl with a lid: soak 1½ cups (250g) of whole-grain couscous in the bowl with two cups of cold water. When absorbed, add three skinned and seeded red bell peppers, grilled asparagus, and two small patty-pan squash and a small bunch of scallions, all chopped finely. Add three good handfuls of chopped fresh herbs (cilantro, mint, and parsley are good) and dress with olive oil and lemon juice, fresh black pepper, and a little salt. Bring plenty of flat breads to go with the meal, plastic bowls and spoons, paper napkins, and water and fruit juice. Afterwards, everyone can eat fresh fruit and the ice-cream you send them up to the ice-cream stand for, while you drink coffee from the thermos.

Now send them all back off down to the sea to wash. Ah, peace at last! Pack all the remainders away, pour yourself another drink, and relax. Now how is he getting on with the sandcastle? Good grief, I wouldn't live in it! Just look at that tilt! Those towers falling already and it was on the market for twenty million. You can tell his day job is architect: all high ideas and leave it to the contractor to sort out the practicalities.

Oh, and the sandwiches? Never.

But this shore will never more be
more attractive than it is now.

HENRY DAVID THOREAU

EXTRACT FROM

American Woman's Home

by

HARRIET AND CATHERINE BEECHER STOWE

In regard to forming habits of obedience, there have been two
extremes, both of which need to be shunned. One is, a stern
and unsympathizing maintenance of parental authority,
demanding perfect and constant obedience, without any
attempt to convince a child of the propriety and benevolence
of the requisitions, and without any manifestation of sympathy
and tenderness for the pain and difficulties which are to be
met. Under such discipline, children grow up to fear their
parents, rather than to love and trust them; while some of
the most valuable principles of character are chilled, or
forever blasted.

In shunning this danger, other parents pass to the opposite
extreme. They put themselves too much on the footing of
equals with their children, as if little were due to superiority
of relation, age, and experience. Nothing is exacted, without
the implied concession that the child is to be a judge of the
propriety of the requisition; and reason and persuasion are
employed, where simple command and obedience would be
far better. This system produces a most pernicious influence.

Children soon perceive the position thus allowed them,
and take every advantage of it. They soon learn to dispute

parental requirements, acquire habits of forwardness and conceit, assume disrespectful manners and address, maintain their views with pertinacity, and yield to authority with ill-humor and resentment, as if their rights were infringed upon.

The medium course is for the parent to take the attitude of a superior in age, knowledge, and relation, who has a perfect right to control every action of the child, and that, too, without giving any reason for the requisitions. "Obey because your parent commands," is always a proper and sufficient reason: though not always the best to give.

But care should be taken to convince the child that the parent is conducting a course of discipline, designed to make him happy; and in forming habits of implicit obedience, self-denial, and benevolence, the child should have the reasons for most requisitions kindly stated; never, however, on the demand of it from the child, as a right, but as an act of kindness from the parent.

It is impossible to govern children properly, especially those of strong and sensitive feelings, without a constant effort to appreciate the value which they attach to their enjoyments and pursuits. A lady of great strength of mind and sensibility once told the writer that one of the most acute periods of suffering in her whole life was occasioned by the burning up of some milkweed-silk, by her mother. The child had found, for the first time, some of this shining and beautiful substance; was filled with delight at her discovery; was arranging it in parcels; planning its future use, and ☞

her pleasure in showing it to her companions—when her mother, finding it strewed over the carpet, hastily swept it into the fire, and that, too, with so indifferent an air, that the child fled away, almost distracted with grief and disappointment. The mother little realized the pain she had inflicted, but the child felt the unkindness so severely that for several days her mother was an object, almost of aversion. While, therefore, the parent needs to carry on a steady course, which will oblige the child always to give up its will, whenever its own good or the greater claims of others require it, this should be constantly connected with the expression of a tender sympathy for the trials and disappointments thus inflicted.

Those, again, who will join with children and help them in their sports, will learn by this mode to understand the feelings and interests of childhood; while at the same time, they secure a degree of confidence and affection which can not be gained so easily in any other way. And it is to be regretted that parents so often relinquish this most powerful mode of influence to domestics and playmates, who often use it in the most pernicious manner.

Next to the want of all government, the two most fruitful sources of evil to children are, unsteadiness in government and over-government. Most of the cases in which the children of sensible and conscientious parents turn out badly, result from one or the other of these causes. In cases of unsteady government, either one parent is very strict, severe and unbending, and the other excessively indulgent, or else the parents are sometimes very strict and decided, and at other times allow disobedience to go unpunished. In such cases, children, never knowing exactly when they can escape with impunity, are constantly tempted to make the trial.

The bad effects of this can be better appreciated by reference to one important principle of the mind. It is found to be universally true, that, when any object of desire is put entirely beyond the reach of hope or expectation, the mind very soon ceases to long for it, and turns to other objects of pursuit. But so long as the mind is hoping for some good, and making efforts to obtain it, any opposition excites irritable feelings. Let the object be put entirely beyond all hope, and this irritation soon ceases.

In consequence of this principle, those children who are under the care of persons of steady and decided government know that whenever a thing is forbidden or denied, it is out of the reach of hope; the desire, therefore, soon ceases, and they turn to other objects. But the children of undecided, or of over-indulgent parents, never enjoy this preserving aid. When a thing is denied, they never know hut either coaxing may win it, or disobedience secure it without any penalty, and so they are kept in that state of hope and anxiety which produces irritation and tempts to insubordination. The children of very indulgent parents, and of those who are undecided and unsteady in government, are very apt to become fretful, irritable, and fractious.

Another class of persons, in shunning this evil, go to the other extreme, and are very strict and pertinacious in regard to every requisition. With them, fault-finding and penalties abound, until the children are either hardened into indifference of feeling, and obtuseness of conscience, or else become excessively irritable or misanthropic.

It demands great wisdom, patience, and self-control, to escape these two extremes. In aiming at this, there are parents who have found the following maxims of very great value:

First: Avoid, as much as possible, the multiplication of rules and absolute commands. Instead of this, take the attitude of advisers. "My child, this is improper, I wish you would remember not to do it." This mode of address answers for all the little acts of heedlessness, awkwardness, or ill-manners so frequently occurring with children. There are cases, when direct and distinct commands are needful; and in such cases, a penalty for disobedience should be as steady and sure as the laws of nature. Where such steadiness and certainty of penalty attend disobedience, children no more think of disobeying than they do of putting their fingers into a burning candle.

The next maxim is, Govern by rewards more than by penalties. Such faults as willful disobedience, lying, dishonesty, and indecent or profane language, should be punished with severe penalties, after a child has been fully instructed in the evil of such practices. But all the constantly recurring faults of the nursery, such as ill-humor, quarreling, carelessness, and ill-manners, may, in a great many cases, be regulated by gentle and kind remonstrances, and by the offer of some reward for persevering efforts to form a good habit.

It is very injurious and degrading to any mind to be kept under the constant fear of penalties. Love and hope are the principles that should be mainly relied on, in forming the habits of childhood.

Another maxim, and perhaps the most difficult, is, Do not govern by the aid of severe and angry tones. A single example will be given to illustrate this maxim. A child is disposed to talk and amuse itself at table. The mother requests it to be silent, except when needing to ask for food, or when spoken to by its older friends. It constantly forgets. The mother, instead of rebuking in an impatient tone, says, "My child, you must remember not to talk. I will remind you of it four times more, and after that, whenever you forget, you must leave the table and wait till we are done." If the mother is steady in her government, it is not probable that she will have to apply this slight penalty more than once or twice.

The writer has been in some families where the most efficient and steady government has been sustained without the use of a cross or angry tone; and in others, where a far less efficient discipline was kept up, by frequent severe rebukes and angry remonstrances. In the first case, the children followed the example set them, and seldom used severe tones to each other; in the latter, the method employed by the parents was imitated by the children, and cross words and angry tones resounded from morning till night, in every portion of the household.

Another important maxim is, Try to keep children in a happy state of mind. Every one knows, by experience, that it is easier to do right and submit to rule when cheerful ☞

and happy, than when irritated. This is peculiarly true of children; and a wise mother, when she finds her child fretful and impatient, and thus constantly doing wrong, will often remedy the whole difficulty, by telling some amusing story, or by getting the child engaged in some amusing sport. This strongly shows the importance of learning to govern children without the employment of angry tones, which always produce irritation.

Children of active, heedless temperament, or those who are odd, awkward, or unsuitable in their remarks and deportment, are often essentially injured by a want of patience and self-control in those who govern them. Such children often possess a morbid sensibility which they strive to conceal, or a desire of love and approbation, which preys like a famine on the soul. And yet, they become objects of ridicule and rebuke to almost every member of the family, until their sensibilities are tortured into obtuseness or misanthropy. Such children, above all others, need tenderness and sympathy. A thousand instances of mistake or forgetfulness should be passed over in silence, while opportunities for commendation and encouragement should be diligently sought.

In regard to the formation of habits of self-denial in childhood, it is astonishing to see how parents who are very sensible often seem to regard this matter. Instead of inuring their children to this duty in early life, so that by habit it may be made easy in after-days, they seem to be studiously seeking to cut them off from every chance to secure such a preparation. Every wish of the child is studiously gratified; and, where a necessity exists of crossing its wishes, some compensating pleasure is offered, in return. Such parents often maintain that nothing shall be put on their table, which their children may not join them in eating. But where, so easily and surely as at the daily meal, can that habit of self-denial be formed?

In forming the moral habits of children, it is wise to take into account the peculiar temptations to which they are to be exposed. The people of this nation are eminently a trafficking people; and the present standard of honesty, as to trade and debts, is very low, and every year seems sinking still lower. It is, therefore, preeminently important, that children should be trained to strict honesty, both in word and deed. It is not merely teaching children to avoid absolute lying, which is needed: all kinds of deceit should be guarded against; and all kinds of little dishonest practices be strenuously opposed. A child should be brought up with the determined principle, never to run in debt, but to be content to live in a humbler way, in order to secure that true independence, which should be the noblest distinction of an American citizen.

There is no more important duty devolving upon a mother, than the cultivation of habits of modesty and propriety in young children. All indecorous words or deportment should be carefully restrained; and delicacy and reserve studiously cherished. It is a common notion, that it is important to secure these virtues to one sex, more than to the other; and, by a strange inconsistency, the sex most exposed to danger is the one selected as least needing care. Yet a wise mother will be especially careful that her sons are trained to modesty and purity of mind.

My mother had a great deal of trouble
with me, but I think she enjoyed it.

MARK TWAIN

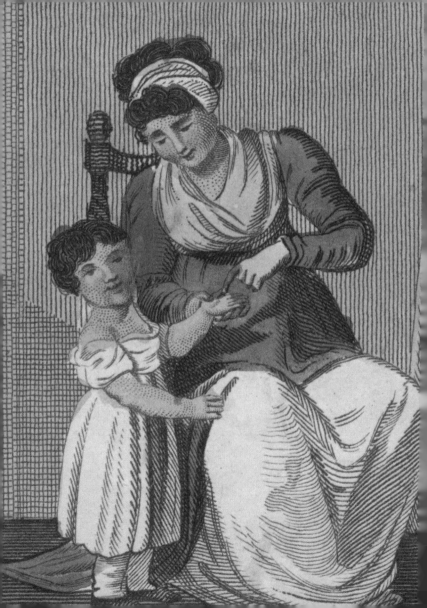

Pat-a-cake

Pat-a-cake, pat-a-cake, baker's man,
Bake me a cake as fast as you can;
Pat it and prick it and mark it with "B,"
And pop in the oven for Baby and me.

* Alternatively, you can use the baby's
first initial and name.

Mother's baking tips

A child never forgets the things he or she learns while cooking with mother. And sometimes it's the little things, the tips and her special ways of doing things, that prove to be of most lasting value. Many such hints have to do with things that are not precisely described in cookbooks—concepts such as "lightness" and "coolness." Mother taught that everything had to be kept cool while making pastry (including tempers), and how to run the inside of the wrists under cold running water to cool the hands. Or how to flour the rolling-pin regularly to stop dough sticking to it, or to drop an ice-cube in the pancake mix to make the batter lighter. Or how to separate an egg by passing the yolk quickly back and forth from one half of the broken shell to the other, while letting the white drop through into a bowl—a magic trick! Or how to keep a cake batter light by using only the very tips of the fingers to rub the fat into the flour.

Mother teaches daughter these semi-mystical secrets in the kitchen and they are passed down from generation to generation. But like all mystique, they, too, may become adrift from reality. One mother taught her daughter to always bend the lower joint of a leg of lamb before roasting—making it an admonition that approached an iron law. When at last the daughter reached the age of reason, she ventured to ask why. The mother had no idea. So then the child asked her grandmother. It seemed that she had once owned a roasting pan that was just a tad too small for the average family roast.

Mama's magic apple pie

Modern mothers thank their lucky stars for ready-made pastry—it tastes fine and saves precious time that you can use for playing with the kids.

Serves 6–8

Frozen pastry for a double-crust pie
9in/23cm pie pan
2–3 tbsp/30–45ml cold water
Milk, for brushing

Filling
$\frac{1}{4}$ cup/55g superfine sugar, plus
  extra for sprinkling
1 tsp/5ml ground cinnamon
2$\frac{1}{4}$lb/1kg dessert apples, peeled, cored,
  and thinly sliced

1 Divide the pastry into two pieces. Roll out one piece on a lightly floured surface into a circle 10 inches (25cm) in diameter and use to line a 9 inch (23 cm) pie pan.

2 Mix together the sugar and cinnamon and sprinkle over the sliced apples. Arrange the apple slices in the pan— don't worry if the apples are above the top of the pan.

3 Roll out the remaining pastry into a circle 10 inches (25 cm) in diameter . Brush the edge of the pastry in the pan with a little milk. Carefully lay the pastry circle over the apples and press down the edges to seal. Trim off any excess pastry and decorate the edge with a fork, if desired. Make two slashes in the top of the pie or prick with a fork a couple of times.

4 Brush the top of the pastry with a little milk, then sprinkle with sugar. Bake in the center of a preheated oven at 400°F/200°C/Gas 6 for 25 to 30 minutes, or until the pastry is golden and the apples tender The pie can be served warm or cold.

Look after yourself!

Because a mother's main role in life is to look after other people, her greatest challenge is to find the time and energy to take care of herself. This is no mean feat. It might involve sitting down for a little while (without someone in your lap), reading a book (yours), going to bed early (yours), or taking time to eat a meal (after it has been fully cooked and put on the table).

The first post-birth hurdle is the strange relationship you seem to have developed with your own body. The new mother soon discovers that it isn't quite all hers any more. At least, baby doesn't think so. Neither is it as she vaguely remembers it before: now there are all kinds of gaps and crinkles which take some getting used to. And then there's the extra weight (oh yes, we all know we're only officially allowed to put on 18–20 pounds [8–9 kilos] for the whole pregnancy, but you try reading the scales over a tummy that size!). Still, this is perfect time to embark on a slender and sound eating routine instead of all that boring and endless dieting.

And although the word "relaxin" may sound like the title of some song that derisively reminds you of a luxury long vanished from the memory of womankind, in fact it is a specific hormone secreted during pregnancy to soften your joints and let the baby grow and emerge more easily. Although relaxin is no longer produced after giving birth, the effects linger for about five months, so to avoid injuries you have to take care with those postnatal exercises. You may begin with very gentle exercises in the first few weeks, but you should have a satisfactory postnatal checkup before doing any more vigorous exercise, and mothers are advised to wait eight to ten weeks after a cesarian section.

After that, you may follow any reputable book or course of exercises, as long as you have the aid of a good supporting bra and sensible footwear. Attending exercise classes can provide truly invaluable moral support from other new mothers. Rest is as beneficial as exercise when you're really tired, and no exercise should be overdone. Strain and pain are stop signs. Pelvic-floor exercises are gentle and really valuable; even though they might not feel as if they are doing much good, they are. And remember, drinking eight glasses of water a day is the simplest and best health and beauty aid.

Just as you start physical exercises gradually and build up over a number of weeks, the same goes for exercises in rebuilding feminine poise. The gentle art of maternal self-preservation is learned step by step. It begins with snatching the time to attend to basic bodily functions (yours) and ends with a long, fragrant soak in the bathtub, a babysitter, and a well-earned evening out. Sharing the caring. That's what it's all about.

Love is patient, love is kind, and is not jealous.

1 COR. 13, BIBLE

Pet loves

Lassie, 101 Dalmatians, Black Beauty— stories of the loving bond between children and animals—have inspired millions of kids. But the reality of having a pet to look after involves demanding lessons in responsibility—the daily feeding and cleaning routine lasts much longer than a film or a book. Animal welfare societies warn, "A dog is not just for Christmas," and it's sad but true—a pet can far outlive childish enthusiasm.

An animal responds to gentle and kind treatment with affection, companionship, and fun. But this, like all other reciprocal relationships, is a serious business. It can even form the foundation for caring for other humans. A pet gives a child the first chance to nurture a creature smaller than him or herself, a neat role reversal—but also a big challenge. It's not unusual for a mother to soon discover that she has somehow adopted a hamster.

It's a revelation for a child to learn that neglect can harm or even kill a living being. So it's a good idea to start slow and small. Goldfish are a perfect first pet, but they don't give much love back. Hamsters are cheap, easy to look after, furry, and fun, but live only for two years and may nip if handled roughly. Also, they're nocturnal, so are most active when the small owner is supposed to be fast asleep. Rabbits are very sociable (keep two!) and guinea pigs can be kept

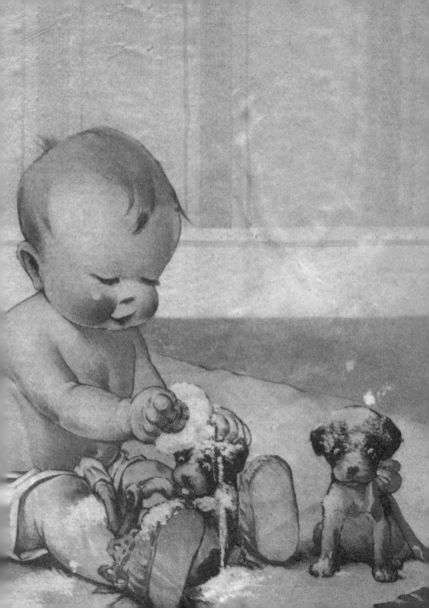

indoors or out in good weather as long as you have a big, movable hutch. Budgies and canaries make chirpy pets. Rats, mice, and gerbils are said to be both intelligent and affectionate. Cats and kittens need lots of love and give lots back but, although independent, they need careful feeding and veterinary care. And dogs, of course, are the biggest favorite of all. A young child will need lots of help caring for a dog, but the rewards are commensurate. A dog, like a mother, gives oodles of unconditional love.

Although human immune-boosting substances are found in cat and dog saliva, children shouldn't share their dinner with their pet. It's also a good idea to wash hands after playing with a pet and avoid contact with animal waste. Asthma and allergies have both been blamed on pets, but research shows that many children who live with cats develop an immune response that actually prevents them from getting asthma. And although approximately two percent of the United States population are allergic to cats, one third of these ignore medical advice and keep at least one feline friend at home.

Caring for a defenceless animal is a life-enhancing exercise in mutual love, so when the relationship ends it can be heartbreaking. The shock and grief of the death of a pet can often be a child's first brush with mortality, so it helps to talk about it in real terms—without too many confusing euphemisms about "falling asleep"—and lots of cuddling to staunch the tears. A burial ceremony is very appropriate—the more dignified and well-attended the better.

Mother Goose

Goosey, goosey, gander,
Whither shall I wander?
Upstairs, and downstairs,
And in my lady's chamber.

Mothers have always recited rhymes and folk stories to their children, but the first collection of fairy tales to be printed under the subtitle "Tales from My Mother Goose" appeared in 1697. The book of ten stories was called *Tales from the Past with Morals* and was published in France, by Charles Perrault.

If there ever was a real Mother Goose, she may have been the 8th-century noblewoman, Bertrada II of Laon, who was the mother of Charlemagne, founder of the Holy Roman Empire. Bertrada, who was a patroness of children and personally educated Charlemagne, was known as Berte aux Grands Pieds, Bertha Greatfoot, or Queen Goosefoot. In France, by the mid-17th century a mythical Mother Goose—Mère l'Oye—was widely believed to be a noble birdmother who told charming tales to children. Many of these spread around Europe and were printed in Italy, then used by both Molière and Shakespeare in their playwriting.

Perrault's book first appeared in English in about 1729 as *Mother Goose's Fairy Tales*. In 1760, John Newberry published three children's books, one of which was entitled *Mother Goose's Melody*. Then, in 1787, Isaiah Thomas was responsible for the first American edition of *Mother Goose's Melody* or *Sonnets for the Cradle* and since then the collection has been expanded to include some 700 rhymes, stories, and riddles.

Oh Dear Mother

Oh dear mother, what a rose I be!
Two young men came a-courting me,
One was blind and the other couldn't see—
Oh dear mother, what a rose I be!

My Mother Said
Never Play With Gypsies

My Mother said, I never should
Play with the gypsies in the wood;
If I did, she would say,
You naughty girl to disobey.
Your hair shan't curl and your shoes shan't shine,
You gypsy girl, you shan't be mine.
And my father said that if I did
He'd rap my head with the teapot-lid.

Mother, May I?

"Mother, may I go out to swim?"
"Yes, my darling daughter.
Fold your clothes up neat and trim,
But don't go near the water."

My Mother And Your Mother

My mother and your mother live across the way.
Every night they have a fight and this is what they say:

Icky bicky soda cracker,
Icky bicky boo.
Icky bicky soda cracker,
Out goes you!

A Vexed Song

Trip upon trenchers,
And dance upon dishes,
My mother sent me for some barm, some barm;
She bid me go lightly,
And come again quickly,
For fear the young men should do me some harm.
Yet didn't you see, yet didn't you see,
What naughty tricks they put upon me?
They broke my pitcher
And spilt the water,
And huffed my mother,
And chid her daughter,
And kissed my sister instead of me.

What shall we read?

There are lots and lots of bestseller lists. A mother looking for a book to give her child nowadays can get pretty intellectual about it and consult the charts, explore the Net, peep to see who's won a literary prize, read the reviews, and follow writers' television appearances. Who doesn't know by now how that most famous modern author of children's books wrote her first wizard ruse on rainy afternoons in a café in some misty Scottish city? It's a magical mystery tale in itself.

Children love to read anything weird and wonderful, strange and half-true, scary and familiar to their own hidden inner world. That's why they've taken *Harry Potter* to their hearts. Before him, they thrived on King Arthur and the Knights of the Round Table, and Merlin, and all the fairy tales of Hans Christian Andersen. They want the dreamy, timeless world of Peter Pan or *The Lion, the Witch and the Wardrobe* by C. S. Lewis and *Charlie and the Chocolate Factory* and all the other titles by Roald Dahl, those perennial, wickedly anti-adult favorites.

For the really little ones, *The Tale of Peter Rabbit* and all Beatrix Potter's other classic offerings are perfect. Monsters always go down well too, including the heffalump in *Winnie-the-Pooh* by A. A. Milne and the newest gruesome ones like *The Gruffalo* by Julia Donaldson. Little people who live underneath the floorboards, like

The Borrowers are very interesting, especially when you know they must exist because precious little things really do disappear. Anything greedy is fun, especially when it's *The Very Hungry Caterpillar* by Eric Carle, with the caterpillar's big, fat, green, hairy tummy that you can see getting bigger and bigger as the pages turn and the pictures go by.

The fantasy world of *Alice in Wonderland* and *Alice Through the Looking Glass* by Lewis Carroll is still a thrill, and so are *The Adventures of Huckleberry Finn* by Mark Twain and *The Railway Children* by E. Nesbit. *The Secret Garden* by Frances Hodgson Burnett provides an enchanting tale of growing up away from grown-up prying—perfect for the dreamy romantic child of twelve …

And then there are some old staple favorites: the books of Dr. Seuss, Theodor Seuss Geisel, born in Springfield, MA in 1904 and an Oxford graduate, who was first persuaded to write a children's book after a report on widespread illiteracy at that time. It was said that children were not reading because their books were "too boring." His publisher sent Geisel a list of 400 important words required by a "first grader" and asked him to cut it to an absorbable 250, and write a book. The result was *The Cat in the Hat*, first published in 1957. Today it's number nine on the top 50 all-time bestselling children's books list. *Green Eggs and Ham* was written using only 50 words, and that's still at number four on the list! So, no excuses for not reading, then!

Reading together

Just when she feels most exhausted, it is time for mother to read a story to her child. And so, overcoming her tiredness, she finds a comfortable place to sit down. Now begins the familiar ritual: a book has to be chosen, fetched, and opened at the right page, as junior snuggles into the perfect place—in her lap or just squeezed in beside her. Then, encircled by mother's arm, there is the wriggling to find a better position for looking at the pictures. But at last, both are settled and the story begins. "Once upon a time…"

It doesn't seem to matter whether the content of the story is classic or contemporary, or made up by mother. "Life itself is the most wonderful fairy tale," said Hans Christian Andersen. Mother's voice is calm and soft and full of truth and her child listens spellbound. Really, it is hard to believe that this is the same mini-whirlwind who raced, yelling, around the room five minutes ago.

Indeed, nothing will break the spell until the story is over and the book closed. And then comes question time. Why was it only a small bear when bears are always big? How do flowers grow? Why do clouds burst?

Questions like these and the answers mother gives will provide invaluable lessons in vocabulary and comprehension, laying the foundation for her child's future literacy skills. "That best academy, a mother's knee," said James Russell Lowell, and although he was certainly right, it might be a bit difficult to trace that exact process from the words of my favorite three-year-old, who declared, "Baba's book is bestest book ever me see!"

One good mother is worth a hundred schoolmasters.

GEORGE HERBERT

EXTRACT FROM

Little Women

by

LOUISA MAY ALCOTT

My dear Mamma,

Having a quiet hour before we leave for Berne, I'll try
to tell you what has happened, for some of it is very
important, as you will see. The sail up the Rhine was
perfect, and I just sat and enjoyed it with all my might.
Get Father's old guidebooks and read about it. I haven't
words beautiful enough to describe it. At Coblenz we had
a lovely time, for some students from Bonn, with whom
Fred got acquainted on the boat, gave us a serenade. It
was a moonlight night, and about one o'clock Flo and I
were waked by the most delicious music under our
windows. We flew up, and hid behind the curtains, but sly
peeps showed us Fred and the students singing away down
below. It was the most romantic thing I ever saw—the river,
the bridge of boats, the great fortress opposite, moonlight
everywhere, and music fit to melt a heart of stone.

When they were done we threw down some flowers, and
saw them scramble for them, kiss their hands to the

invisible ladies, and go laughing away, to smoke and drink beer, I suppose. Next morning Fred showed me one of the crumpled flowers in his vest pocket, and looked very sentimental. I laughed at him, and said I didn't throw it, but Flo, which seemed to disgust him, for he tossed it out of the window, and turned sensible again. I'm afraid I'm going to have trouble with that boy, it begins to look like it.

The baths at Nassau were very gay, so was Baden-Baden, where Fred lost some money, and I scolded him. He needs someone to look after him when Frank is not with him. Kate said once she hoped he'd marry soon, and I quite agree with her that it would be well for him. Frankfurt was delightful. I saw Goethe's house, Schiller's statue, and Dannecker's famous *Ariadne*. It was very lovely, but I should have enjoyed it more if I had known the story better. I didn't like to ask, as everyone knew it or pretended they did. I wish Jo would tell me all about it. I ought to have read more, for I find I don't know anything, and it mortifies me.

Now comes the serious part, for it happened here, and Fred has just gone. He has been so kind and jolly that we all got quite fond of him. I never thought of anything but a traveling friendship till the serenade night. Since then I've begun to feel that the moonlight walks, balcony talks, and daily adventures were something more to him than fun. I haven't flirted, Mother, truly, but remembered what you said to me, and have done my very best. I can't help it if people like me. I don't try to make them, and it worries me if I don't care for them, though Jo says I haven't got any heart. Now I know Mother will shake her head, and the girls say, "Oh, the mercenary little wretch!" but I've made up my mind, and if Fred asks me, I shall accept him, though I'm not madly in love. I like him, and we get on comfortably together. He is handsome, young, clever enough, and very rich—ever much richer than the Laurences. I don't think his family would object, and I should be very happy, for they are all kind, well-bred, generous people, and they like me. Fred, as the eldest twin, will have the estate, I suppose, and such a splendid one it is! A city house in a fashionable street, not so showy as our big houses, but twice as comfortable and full of solid luxury, such as English people believe in. I like it, for it's genuine. I've seen the plate, the family jewels, the old servants, and pictures of the country place, with its park, great house, lovely grounds, and fine horses. Oh, it would be all I should ask!

And I'd rather have it than any title such as girls snap up so readily, and find nothing behind. I may be mercenary, but I hate poverty, and don't mean to bear it a minute longer than I can help. One of us must marry well. Meg didn't, Jo won't, Beth can't yet, so I shall, and make everything okay all round. I wouldn't marry a man I hated or despised. You may be sure of that, and though Fred is not my model hero, he does very well, and in time I should get fond enough of him if he was very fond of me, and let me do just as I liked. So I've been turning the matter over in my mind the last week, for it was impossible to help seeing that Fred liked me. He said nothing, but little things showed it. He never goes with Flo, always gets on my side of the carriage, table, or promenade, looks sentimental when we are alone, and frowns at anyone else who ventures to speak to me. Yesterday at dinner, when an Austrian officer stared at us and then said something to his friend, a rakish-looking baron, about 'ein wonderschönes Blondchen,' Fred looked as fierce as a lion, and cut his meat so savagely it nearly flew off his plate. He isn't one of the cool, stiff Englishmen, but is rather peppery, for he has Scotch blood in him, as one might guess from his bonnie blue eyes. 👉

Well, last evening we went up to the castle about sunset, at least all of us but Fred, who was to meet us there after going to the Post Restante for letters. We had a charming time poking about the ruins, the vaults where the monster tun is, and the beautiful gardens made by the elector long ago for his English wife. I liked the great terrace best, for the view was divine, so while the rest went to see the rooms inside, I sat there trying to sketch the gray stone lion's head on the wall, with scarlet woodbine sprays hanging round it. I felt as if I'd got into a romance, sitting there, watching the Meckar rolling through the valley, listening to the music of the Austrian band below, and waiting for my lover, like a real storybook girl. I had a feeling that something was going to happen and I was ready for it. I didn't feel blushy or quakey, but quite cool and only a little excited.

By-and-by I heard Fred's voice, and then he came hurrying through the great arch to find me. He looked so troubled that I forgot all about myself, and asked what the matter was. He said he'd just got a letter begging him to come home, for Frank was very ill. So he was going at once on the night train and only had time to say good-bye. I was very sorry for him, and disappointed for myself, but only for a minute because he said, as he shook hands, and said it in a way that I could not mistake, "I shall soon come back, you won't forget me, Amy?"

I didn't promise, but I looked at him, and he seemed satisfied, and there was no time for anything but messages and good-byes, for he was off in an hour, and we all miss him very much. I know he wanted to speak, but I think, from something he once hinted, that he had promised his father not to do anything of the sort yet a while, for he is a rash boy, and the old gentleman dreads a foreign daughter-in-law. We shall soon meet in Rome, and then, if I don't change my mind, I'll say "Yes, thank you," when he says "Will you, please?"

Of course this is all very private, but I wished you to know what was going on. Don't be anxious about me, remember I am your 'prudent Amy,' and be sure I will do nothing rashly. Send me as much advice as you like. I'll use it if I can. I wish I could see you for a good talk, Marmee. Love and trust me.

Ever your

Amy

With a wave of a wand...

"I'm going to be the fairy in the school play!" announces the little one in great excitement. And before she knows where she is, mother has joined her daughter in the fantasy! For as if by magic, there has to appear a starry wand, a sparkly dress, and, of course, fairy wings. This will all require time, effort, glue, stitch-witchery, and glitter, but somewhere inside each mother there's a little girl who once wanted to be a fairy too…so this is her moment to enjoy a second chance.

A toy box full of old clothes gives a host of alter egos for a child. Add feathers, veils, or badges to old hats. You can easily make a tall, pointy, witch's hat from a cardboard cone, and a crown from a circle of stiff paper covered with glitter. A length of silky material with a button at the neck becomes a cloak or cape. Any of mother's old summer skirts makes a gypsy outfit, and an old stripy tee shirt with some scarves and a black eyepatch turns anyone into a pirate. Swashbuckling daggers and swords should be of flexible silver paper so that nobody gets hurt.

Actually, a dress-up box is nothing so prosaic as a mere storage container; it's really a Pandora's Box that gives children entry to the world of make-believe. Nothing beats the pleasure and enrichment of changing persona at will, and nothing is so stimulating for the developing imagination. This is how future actors and actresses begin—devising a play, rehearsing it in secret, and then inviting parents to sit and watch the performance.

And the fairy godmother? Well, today that's you!

THE DRESS-UP BOX

A dress-up box makes wonderful mother magic. It serves the dual purpose of emptying mother's wardrobe of all the stuff she can't bear to give to the thrift shop and at the same time fills her child's head with creative ideas. The dress-up box is a repository for precious articles that mother can't possibly part with because a) she got married in it, b) she nearly got married in it, c) it reminds her of being a carefree student, and a certain handsome date, d) she found it in the Ladies' Room at that grand hotel, or e) she would get rid of it, but she knows it absolutely must go in the dress-up box.

The final point covers a whole lot of wonderful things. The hat she wore when she was her best friend's chief bridesmaid. And the one she wore when she was her other best friend's chief bridesmaid. And her old riding hat. And her old straw gardening hat. And father's old cowboy Stetson and uncle's funny battered felt trilby. There are scarves, belts, rings, and strings of things that look like beads, and bow ties granddad threw away and ordinary ties that father didn't really throw away but mother did, and his old shirt and her old white blouse, which is for pirates, with boots and a sword…

There are old skirts and a complete old suit from the other granddad, with wide lapels and stripes, and that's for being Al

Capone in, or any other gangster dude (with a plastic pistol). There's a marching jacket from the thrift shop—bought, this time, for just two dollars, with gilt buttons, and that's for being a soldier (with a drum). There are two old silky dressing gowns with tasseled belts, for the robes of a king and a queen (which just need cardboard crowns).

There's camouflage for fighting in the jungle; some old trousers from when father was into combat gear—that's when he was young—and a couple of weird old floppy hats that people wore in the sun. These are all great for action-hero-type games and making camps outside.

There are a lot of accessories for dressing things up even more, and for plays that require old-fashioned costumes. Belts, ribbons, clips, badges and brooches, buttons and bows, sparkly, glittery, sequin collars and cuffs—all these are kept in another box inside the dress-up box. An old beaten-up suitcase houses magic tricks. Long scraps of material, especially silky ones, make great capes. Velvet dresses, floaty veils, feathers, and artificial flowers all have a role to play.

The wise mother also collects things that help: cardboard boxes, tubes, silver and gold paper, black poster board, drinking straws, thin sticks, popsicle-sticks, yogurt containers, and various plastic containers. These are for robots, knights in armor, helmets, swords, crowns, emblems…all that sort of thing. You get the general idea, mom!

Home talent furnished stars, stock
company, orchestra, and scene painter;
and astonishing performances were
given on this pretty little stage.

LOUISA MAY ALCOTT

Making music

Long before he's old enough to have his own band, your child will want to be in one and will ask for a guitar. This appears to be a normal stage in becoming a normal human being. Music seems to play a significant role in our development. One thing is sure, every child has a natural inclination to bang, blow, jingle, and sing—sort of—and nursery rhymes and songs are only the start.

So in advance of the Stratocaster with its fast-action maple neck, comfort-contoured body, and bullet truss rod—well, you can bet Jimi Hendrix knew what one was—you can get an amazing band together at a much lower cost. And this is a good plan, because incipient musicians of three upwards who have been influenced by early Hendrix can be nearly as wild on stage as he was, and Stratocasters are not cheap.

Make a tambourine by stapling two paper plates together, facing each other. Using a hole-punch, make holes around the plates and tie jingle bells to the holes with string or colored yarn. Decorate with ribbons and crayoned colors.

An round box with a lid makes a superb drum. First decorate the box with construction paper and/or crayons. Place the cover on the box. Use a pen to make a hole in the center of the bottom and the center of the cover, and thread with a piece of yarn that's long enough to hang around the child's neck and down to his or her waist. For drumsticks, glue two empty wooden thread spools to the end of pencils.

For a horn, cover one end of an empty paper towel roll with waxed paper and secure it with a rubber band. Punch a row of holes along one side of the roll with the tip of a pen. To play, sing a tune into the open end of the horn.

Cymbals can be made using two matching pot covers and some ribbon. Tie the ribbon around the handles of the pot covers and strike together to play. Ouch!

To make a comb buzzer, fold tissue paper over the teeth of a comb. To play, hum through the tissue paper.

To make hand bells, punch a hole in each end of an empty paper towel roll and tie two jingle bells to each side of the roll by running string or yarn through the holes and carefully tying off.

On page 184 you will find instructions for a water xylophone.

A guitar can be fashioned from an empty shoebox with rubber bands stretched around it. Attach a ruler to the back of the box, at one end, to act as the neck of the guitar. To play, strum or pluck the rubber bands.

Here then is an introduction to the whole Stratocaster business, a never-to-be-forgotten era—excuse the pun. To really encourage the first band, make a recording of them—retire gracefully into another room meanwhile. CDs and celebrity come later.

…the heart of me weeps to belong
To the old Sunday evenings at home, with winter outside
And hymns in the cozy parlor, the tinkling piano our guide.

D. H. LAWRENCE

Fun Project: 3
Water xylophone

You will need

- 6 glass bottles of similar size
- Raffia and string scraps
- Blue and green ink or food coloring
- Jug
- Glue
- Assorted shells and beads
- Fine wire scraps
- Metal spoon
- Scissors
- Water

Making a water xylophone

1 Glue beads or shells onto the bottles, or thread beads and shells on string or raffia and hang these around the necks of the bottles.

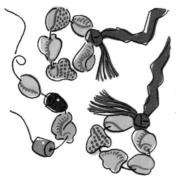

2 For shell tassels, thread shells on wire, twist the wire around the ends of the raffia, and tie the raffia around the bottle neck.

3 Add ink or food coloring to a jar of water. Use less or more ink/food coloring to get different depths of color.

4 Line up the bottles. Pour a little water into the first bottle, more in the next, and so on. The last bottle should be nearly full.

186

Colored glass bottles can be filled with plain water.

The Band

Bring the comb and play upon it!   Marching, here we come!

Willie cocks his highland bonnet,   Johnny beats the drum.

CLAP HANDS AND DANCE

Dancing is the most joyful and natural game for a mother and child. It's lots of fun, of course, and, like all the best things in life, happens spontaneously and by mutual agreement. In any case, all the scientific research concerning the effect of music on human development points to its extraordinary value. We now know that babies listen to music from the outside world while still in the womb, and the sooner infants are introduced to it after birth the better, apparently, for their development.

So we would seem to be instinctively musical creatures. And, like music, we depend on counterpoint for our character. Growing up to belong to other people and society depends upon mirroring, that is to say, the way a child sees himself in other important people's eyes—most significantly mother's. Perhaps this is where dance comes in; when mother and child look into each other's eyes, follow each other's body movements, and mold their bodies to each other, moving in time together to the music. Mother's voice softens and modulates itself to the music… and so the beat goes on, bonding the dancers as it goes. Rhythm expresses a thousand feelings. It binds body, spirit, and mind in a language transcending speech. Mother and child get to know one another in new ways through dance, for every human being moves uniquely. Researchers have discovered the positive results of mother/child dance therapy. So perhaps a child can feel how happy mother is by the tone of her tango!

Laundry day

... five, six, seven, eight, nine,
hang your washing on the line.

Helping mother with the laundry was a normal daughterly duty before the days of washing machines. The task took all day, traditionally a Monday, and that's why a "wet Monday" was dreaded. Children still love doing their doll's laundry while mother hangs the clothes out to dry in the fresh air. This is still a popular alternative to the electric dryer for people with yards. Today, most family laundry is done at the click of a switch, but there will always be fabrics that benefit from being washed by hand.

In 1904, the very first washing machine was invented, and in 1908, the Hurley Machine Company of Chicago marketed an electric one. The first automatic washing machine arrived in Europe in 1951, marking the beginning of the end of washday drudgery. Gone suddenly were the days of outdoor laundering in tin tubs with soap and washboard— these were now gleefully donated to skiffle bands.

But white laundry, including babies' diapers, continued to be cleaned by more traditional methods. It was soaked in a bleach solution and then hygienically boiled in a copper boiler with a central agitator. The laundry had to be hauled out with large wooden tongs, rinsed, and put through a wringer or mangle: very hard work! A wringer had two horizontal rubber rollers and the distance between them was just large enough for an article of wet laundry to pass through it. The rollers were tightened and a handle turned to squeeze the water out of the laundry, ready for the line. Finally, the washing was hung out, using handmade wooden clothes pegs with little round heads.

Add a little household glycerin to a soap and water solution, then blow it through an old clay pipe, wire ring or any perforated object. The result? Globes of rainbows drifting off into the air…

Working mothers

Working mothers are the fastest-growing segment of the workforce, but that doesn't mean they're all happy about it. Whether they have to work or want to work, love their work or hate it, almost all suffer from some conflict and guilt. Children also feel divided about sharing mother with her employer. Mothers and kids like to be together.

The stress when you work both inside and outside the home is considerable, and that's on top of the stressed lifestyle we all lead. Forty-five percent of parents in a recent report stated that they felt they "always" or "most of the time" had to rush to get everything done in the day. The support of a partner makes a great difference, as does that of the employer. Companies offering flextime and child-care services to working mothers have happier, healthier, more committed employees.

But when time at home is limited, the quality of time shared with children becomes crucial. Spillover from work can be positive or negative. A happy mother is a good mother, and there's nothing new in that idea; the ancient Chinese *Tao Te Ching* advises, "In work, do what you enjoy. In family life, be completely present." Many mothers work not only for the money but also for the self-esteem it gives, the autonomy, challenge, and enrichment. So it comes down more to HOW you work rather than IF you work. If you come home fired up with enthusiasm and energy, everyone is going to feel the benefit.

Once home, the thing is to stretch time, sharing most of it with the children. Priorities have to be set here, so this is where workplace skills literally come home to roost. For example, there's "focused" time: talk, discussion, listening, and shared activities. It's so bonding just listening to one another, learning what's going on in one another's lives. A child needs to talk about everything that happened at school that day. If a mother also shares things about her working day—the funny remarks, the child-friendly anecdotes—that gives a real sense of what she does all day, and plants the seed that work can be nice. Children with a constantly complaining, tired, and stressed parent can soon pick up the idea that work is pure hell. At that point, leaving them all day to go and do it can seem like a double insult.

As well as focused time, there's "hang-around" time, where nobody is doing anything very much but doing it together. One person might be doing homework at the kitchen table while mother cooks. Or everyone can just laze around in the same room. You don't have to be engaged in intensive interaction, as the psychologists put it—just enjoy one another's presence on the planet. Be cool and chill out!

In other words, as one young respondent told researchers, "If a child has something to say, listen to them. They might teach you something."

There Was An Old Woman

There was an old woman

Who lived in a shoe,

She had so many children

She didn't know what to do.

She gave them some broth

Without any bread,

Whipped them all soundly

And sent them to bed!

Playing mother

Playing with dolls is a time-honored way for little girls to practice being mother, and watching them play gives their mothers a perfect opportunity to see what they do and how! So everyone benefits! Many a mother is amazed at how well her daughter plays this game, despite having been proudly brought up to eschew a traditional female role.

It is in the blood it seems, and it is interesting to note how the emancipation of women has been accompanied by concurrent regression in the sophistication of some popular brands of doll. These have been growing younger over time, so that now baby dolls have attained helpless infancy, wetting their diapers and crying to be fed.

Dolls have been playthings since the beginning of civilization and have been found in Chinese burial sites dating from 3000BC. At first they were religious objects, but in the early 15th century they began to be commercially produced as children's toys. The 1800s saw the emergence of dolls that looked like little girls or babies—the *bébé*—whereas until then they had all been modeled on adults. The Victorians even devised the "Sunday Only" doll, to be played with only under strict supervision!

By the 1900s, engagingly realistic European baby dolls were being made with painted porcelain or bisque heads, and in 1865, the first American doll-manufacturing company was established. "Kewpie," born in 1913, was one of the first American character dolls, based on drawings by Rosie O'Neill in the 1909 *Ladies' Home Journal*.

EXTRACT FROM

Snow White

by

THE BROTHERS GRIMM

Once upon a time in the middle of winter, when the flakes of
snow were falling like feathers from the sky, a queen sat at a
window sewing, and the frame of the window was made of
black ebony. And whilst she was sewing and looking out of
the window at the snow, she pricked her finger with the
needle, and three drops of blood fell upon the snow. And the
red looked pretty upon the white snow, and she thought to
herself, "Would that I had a child as white as snow, as red as
blood, and as black as the wood of the window-frame."

Soon after that she had a little daughter, who was as white
as snow, and as red as blood, and her hair was as black as
ebony; and she was therefore called Snow White. And when
the child was born, the Queen died.

After a year had passed the King took to himself another
wife. She was a beautiful woman, but proud and haughty, and
she could not bear that anyone else should surpass her in
beauty. She had a wonderful looking-glass, and when she
stood in front of it and looked at herself in it, and said— ☞

👉 "Looking-glass, looking-glass, on the wall,

Who in this land is the fairest of all?" The looking-glass answered—

"Thou, O Queen, art the fairest of all!"

Then she was satisfied, for she knew that the looking-glass spoke the truth.

But Snow White was growing up, and grew more and more beautiful; and when she was seven years old she was as beautiful as the day, and more beautiful than the Queen herself. And once when the Queen asked her looking-glass—

"Looking-glass, looking-glass, on the wall,

Who in this land is the fairest of all?" it answered—

"Thou art fairer than all who are here, Lady Queen."

But more beautiful still is Snow White, as I ween."

Then the Queen was shocked, and turned yellow and green with envy. From that hour, whenever she looked at Snow White, her heart heaved in her breast, she hated the girl so much.

And envy and pride grew higher and higher in her heart like a weed, so that she had no peace day or night. She called a huntsman, and said, "Take the child away into the forest; I will no longer have her in my sight. Kill her, and bring me back her heart as a token." The huntsman obeyed, and took her away; but when he had drawn his knife, and was about to pierce Snow White's innocent heart, she began to weep, and said, "Ah dear huntsman, leave me my life! I will run away into the wild forest, and never come home again."

And as she was so beautiful the huntsman had pity on her and said, "Run away, then, you poor child." "The wild beasts will soon have devoured you," thought he, and yet it seemed as if a stone had been rolled from his heart since it was no longer needful for him to kill her. And as a young boar just then came running by he stabbed it, and cut out its heart and took it to the Queen as proof that the child was dead. The cook had to salt this, and the wicked Queen ate it, and thought she had eaten the heart of Snow White.

But now the poor child was all alone in the great forest, and so terrified that she looked at every leaf of every tree, and did not know what to do. Then she began to run, and ran over sharp stones and through thorns, and the wild beasts ran past her, but did her no harm.

She ran as long as her feet would go until it was almost evening; then she saw a little cottage and went into it to rest herself. Everything in the cottage was small, but neater and cleaner than can be told...As she was so tired, she laid herself down on one of the little beds...one was too long, another too short, but at last she found that the seventh one was right, and so she remained in it, said a prayer and went to sleep.

Mother's Day

A picture memory brings to me,
I look across the years and see
Myself beside my mother's knee.

JOHN GREENLEAF WHITTIER

The sweetest feeling for a mother is being told that she is "the best mom in the world!" And on Mother's Day, millions of mothers hear just those words from their children. The wonder of it is that the message does not seem to be the least bit diluted by multiplication.

The earliest tributes to mothers were made by the ancient Greeks at their spring festival dedicated to Rhea, the mother of many deities. The Romans made offerings to their Mother of Gods, Cybele. In the 1660s, Christians in Britain celebrated this festival on the fourth Sunday of Lent in honor of Mary, Mother of Christ, calling this day Mothering Sunday, and honoring it with a special simnel cake.

Nearly 150 years ago in the United States, Anna Jarvis called for a "Mother's Work Day" to raise awareness of poor health conditions in her Appalachian community. Fifteen years later, Boston poet, pacifist and suffragist Julia Ward Howe held a mothers' rally for peace.

When Anna Jarvis died in 1905, her daughter, also named Anna, began to lobby for a special day just for women, in honor of her mother. White carnations, her mother's favorite flowers, are still worn on Mother's Day. Later Anna, enraged by the commercialization of Mother's Day, filed a lawsuit to abolish it. But by then the idea had thoroughly caught on, and who would want to miss it now? Not this mother!

Homemade lemonade

All summer long, keep pitchers of this refreshing, zingy thirst-quencher in your refrigerator—the children will love it.

Preparation time: 10 minutes

> 4 unwaxed lemons, quartered
> 6oz/175g granulated sugar
> 6 cups/1.5 liters water
> Ice cubes and lemon slices, to serve

1 Place the lemons in a blender or food processor with the sugar and 1¼ cups/300ml water. Process for a few seconds until the lemons are finely chopped.

2 Pour the mixture through a strainer. Add the remaining water and stir well. Add ice cubes and a few extra lemon slices before serving.

Hot chocolate

This soothing drink fills everyone with a comforting warmth on a winter's day; it's a real luxury, especially when made with good-quality semisweet chocolate and whole milk. For extra indulgence, place a spoonful of whipped heavy cream on top of each mug.

Serves 4
Preparation time: 5 minutes   **Cooking time: 2 minutes**

2½ cups/600ml whole milk

2 cinnamon sticks

5oz/150g semisweet chocolate (at least 70% cocoa solids) broken into pieces

½ cup/125ml heavy cream, whipped (optional)

1 Place the milk with the cinnamon sticks in a pan and bring to a boil. Remove from the heat and add the chocolate; stir until melted.

2 Remove the cinnamon sticks and pour the hot chocolate into four mugs. Top each one with 1 tbsp whipped heavy cream, if using, and serve immediately.

SHY BABY!

Shy one, shy one,
Shy one of my heart

WILLIAM BUTLER YEATS

The mother of a very shy youngster feels torn between dispatching her offspring into a world that may hurt, and knowing that her child cannot remain at home forever. Her anguish matches that of the child who dreads teasing and rejection by other children but at the same time longs to join in all the fun and games. It's good to know that shyness is not a disease; it's a "dis-ease"—simply the discomfort of one who takes life seriously.

A "thinker" may appear unfriendly and aloof. In fact, the opposite is usually true, and the timid child is in an agony of uncertainty: how to join in? Lots of positive feedback about all the child's strong character traits works wonders here, plus time to learn confidence skills without pressure. It's also useful to know that at least fifty percent of people describe themselves as shy—and these include some surprisingly successful and famous people, for instance, Robert Frost, Eleanor Roosevelt, Winston Churchill, Barbara Walters, Johnny Carson, and David Letterman.

It seems that the blond, blue-eyed angel may be the last to fly. One psychologist has found a correlation between typical Caucasian coloring and shyness: when people migrated to colder northern European climes, they had trouble maintaining body temperature. They mutated to increase levels of a certain warming, but pigment-inhibiting, biochemical and this left them not only blonder but also much less bold.

Safe with mother

A mother is one to whom you hurry when you are troubled.
EMILY DICKINSON

It is only when a woman becomes a mother that she fully realizes what a frightening place the world can be. And then she has to pretend it isn't. "Keep your fears to yourself, but share your courage with others," said Robert Louis Stevenson, and the greatest test of this comes when a child is clinging to your hand for dear life and you yourself are shaking.

"Small child, small worries," goes the Dutch epigram, "the bigger the child, the greater the worry." While he is still in her arms, the mother worries about her baby's health—but these cares are nothing to the anxiety that begins with the toddler's first steps. It is the beginning of the "No" era, when the word "tired" takes on new meaning for mother as she foresees every catastrophe, moves everything to "above baby reach" height, and runs constantly after an escapee intent on danger.

But as Lao Tse affirmed, "The longest journey starts with a single step" and after that, well, life is a great adventure!

Just you and me

There are plenty of downsides to being a single mother, but what about the upsides? You've got your child all to yourself to enjoy, plenty of gorgeous quality time, and you don't even have to feel guilty about not sharing it with another parent. And children are resilient. They can survive in all kinds of family and non-family situations, so there is no point in worrying about life as a single mother. We all know how much better and more balanced it is to have two parents around. But life doesn't always turn out that way.

As provider, protector, and nurturer, you have a few things to keep you busy. So it isn't a surprise that all the emotions that rise up can come as just a bit too much of a challenge. Children don't like missing a parent, and they don't mind telling you so. But you're missing someone, too. Children don't like taking orders from just one disciplinarian, and they don't mind telling you so. But you're missing some support, too. The moods, morale, and behavior of children and mothers often rise, fall, and clash in something less than unison. And just to add the finishing touch, single mothers often have financial and work issues to face.

There are a few tips…
• A single mother's own reality and needs are important.
• Help is there for the asking, and a list of resources is handy.

216

- All unnecessary chores can be eliminated to make way for a simple life.
- Time alone each day is good, and so is time spent in physical exercise: a brisk walk with your child is perfect.
- Keeping a diary helps to track progress, or the lack of it!
- Coping strategies and experience can be shared with other single mothers.
- Children's response to being fatherless varies, so they can come home with tricky questions, behavioral problems, or school difficulties. Be prepared.
- Even sad feelings can be shared between children and mother.
- Contact with lots of two-parent families is a good idea.
- Childcare can be shared with another single parent so you can get out alone sometimes.
- It's best not to take a date home at first, or even discuss him.
- Badmouthing your child's father goes down very badly and disturbs the lines of communication, which need to be kept open.
- Counseling and help are there for people who might need them, including single mothers.

But in the end, it's up to the single mother to find her own way through it all. And she does. According to recent research, the children of single mothers generally get on very well in life, thank you. So no agonizing over the missing bits! Anyway, children have a funny way of sorting themselves out, once you've stopped looking.

My mother had a slender, small body, but a large heart—a heart so large that everybody's joys found welcome in it, and hospitable accommodation.

MARK TWAIN

Head nurse

There's one thing worse for a mother than being sick herself, and that's having an sick child—one who's really sick, not just trying to get the day off school. But how does she tell? Even avoidance of a history exam can produce quite a subtle bunch of symptoms. Quite violent, sneezing, coughing, and a runny nose can all result from stress, and the symptoms are no less real. So, alert diagnosis, common sense, and reassurance all have a role to play in assessing a child's illness.

If there are scary symptoms, the doctor should be called. Even problems associated with so-called "normal" development, such as teething, can come into this category. High fever, vomiting, diarrhea, and reddened or painful ears, are definitely not just "teething troubles." Fluid loss is always a big issue because babies and young children become dehydrated very quickly.

Ordinary colds, coughs, and childhood complaints can completely ground a child. On the other hand, it's amazing how quickly they recover. One minute your toddler is flat out in bed and you're frantic with worry; the next minute the little tyke is up and about and mischief-making, and all you feel is nostalgia for the former peace and quiet.

As soon as "stay in bed at home" is prescribed, mother-love is the wonder medicine. This consists of lots of attention. Simple comfort measures are a freshly made bed, a hot-water bottle, and a tidy, bright, and well-aired bedroom. Cool, clean hands and face are soothing for both patient and nurse. Plenty of fluids is the golden rule, preferably hourly drinks of water or fresh fruit juice. Sweet, fizzy stuff just makes the little invalid bloated. Fresh fruit can be cut up into "boats" for a bedside snack. In general, keep things simple in the food department: "Feed a cold and starve a fever" was grandmother's sound advice. Appetite and energy should soon come bounding back, setting their own agenda for recovery.

Having his or her temperature taken regularly makes junior feel important, while you can collect useful information. Getting to the bathroom or shower can be a wobbly experience when feverish: a chaperone helps mitigate the "watery knees" effect and is a good ploy for checking up on the quantity and quality of materials exiting the patient. The doctor, if called, invariably wants to know about these things.

Children find it really hard to stay in bed, so the minute they begin to feel better they will try to escape outside or engage in combat with video games or siblings. But sometimes rest or night-time sleeping patterns have to be restored and this is where good old-fashioned methods work best. In fact, the best thing about being sick as a child is lying cosily in bed with mother reading to you—your very own private Florence Nightingale.

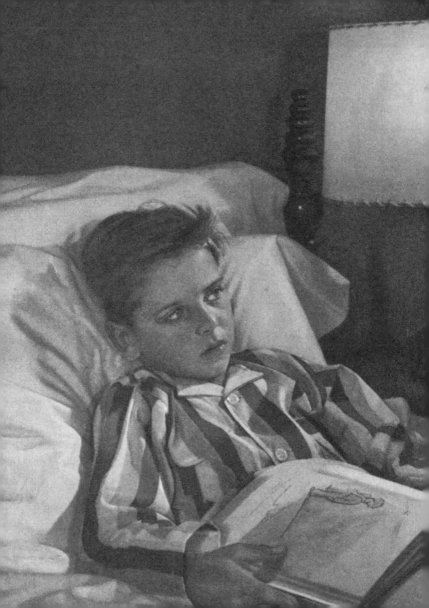

A sick child is always the mother's property:
her own feelings generally make it so.

JANE AUSTEN, *PERSUASION*

Can I get into your bed?

When the bedroom door slowly opens in the middle of the night and a small person creeps across the floor and climbs into mother's bed, how could she refuse? We all remember how it was to wake up from a bad dream all alone and wonder where we are. Nothing is cozier or more comforting for a child than to cuddle up close to mother when it's all dark and things have gone "bump" in the night.

However much people discuss the pros and cons of "co-sleeping," in fact this is exactly what parents and children all over the world have always done, either from lack of space or simply by tradition. Children often sleep in hammocks slung above the parent's bed, or have a crib or futon in the same room.

Most mothers know intuitively when they should take their child into bed with them, how long she should stay there, and why. Many affirm the mutual comfort and improved sleep that comes from the swift meeting of infant needs—resulting in the enhanced sense of security that comes from sharing a bed.

And although some commentators talk about the danger of smothering, others are far less alarmist. Indeed, some experts emphasize that breast-feeding mothers naturally adopt a safe sleeping position. Most children seem happy to return to their own beds once—in their view—their fears have passed. Meanwhile, every child knows that mother's bed is the softest, sweetest, and safest place of all.

Sad and blue

What precious drops are those,
Which silently each other's tracks pursue,
Bright as young diamonds in their faintest dew?

JOHN DRYDEN

As her child sobs helplessly in floods of tears, mother feels mortified.
Her child is so helpless in grief, so lost, so difficult to reach. However
much she asks questions to try to find out what has happened, there is
nothing for it but to wait. The moment will come when she will be
allowed to put her arms around her child and hold him or her close.
And then the sobbing will subside. And then will come the words.

The real challenge may be to understand an apparent discrepancy
between stimulus and response. As adults we are vain enough to
suppose that our tears come in graceful and proper proportion to a
grief, as if this matters, or as if emotion must be dignified by mathematics.
Children have no such inhibitions and will weep equally convincingly at
any event that strikes them as sad, whether it's the demise of a pet
hamster or someone looking at them in an odd way at school.

The most comforting thing is to be taken into mother's arms. This is
where experiences may really be shared, for mother's open, matching
sadness is greatly prized at such moments. So are her empathetic tears,
which may produce an almost magical effect. For if mother can cry the
situation must be sad, and why is mother crying? Thus the questioning
game gets turned on its head and both are suddenly vulnerable to each
other. Which is, after all, an important part of what sadness is all about.

Prelude

by

KATHERINE MANSFIELD

The two left in the kitchen were quiet for a little. Linda leaned her cheek on her fingers and watched her mother. She thought her mother looked wonderfully beautiful with her back to the leafy window. There was something comforting in the sight of her that Linda felt she could never do without. She needed the sweet smell of her flesh, and the soft feel of her cheeks and her arms and shoulders still softer. She loved the way her hair curled, silver at her forehead, lighter at her neck, and bright brown still in the big coil under the muslin cap. Exquisite were her mother's hands, and the two rings she wore seemed to melt into her creamy skin. And she was always so fresh, so delicious. The old woman could bear nothing but linen next to her body and she bathed in cold water winter and summer.

"Isn't there anything for me to do?" asked Linda.

"No, darling. I wish you would go into the garden and give an eye to your children; but that I know you will not do."

"Of course I will, but you know Isabel is much more grown up than any of us."

"Yes, but Kezia is not," said Mrs. Fairfield.

"Oh, Kezia has been tossed by a bull hours ago," said Linda, winding herself up in her shawl again.

But no, Kezia had seen a bull through a hole in a knot of wood in the paling that separated the tennis lawn from the paddock.

But she had not liked the bull frightfully, so she had walked away back through the orchard, up the grassy slope, along the path by the lace-bark tree and so into the spread tangled garden. She did not believe that she would ever not get lost in this garden. Twice she had found her way back to the big iron gates they had driven through the night before, and then had turned to walk up the drive that led to the house, but there were so many little paths on either side. On one side they all led into a tangle of tall dark trees and strange bushes with flat velvet leaves and feathery cream flowers that buzzed with flies when you shook them—this was the frightening side, and no garden at all. The little paths here were wet and clayey with tree roots spanned across them like the marks of big fowls' feet.

But on the other side of the drive there was a high box border and the paths had box edges and all of them led into a deeper and deeper tangle of flowers. The camellias were in bloom, white and crimson and pink and white striped with flashing leaves. You could not see a leaf on the syringa bushes for the white clusters. The roses were in flower—gentlemen's button-hole roses, little white ones, but far too full of insects to hold under anyone's nose, pink monthly roses with a ring of fallen petals round the bushes, cabbage roses on thick stalks, moss roses, always in bud, pink smooth beauties opening curl on curl, red ones so dark they seemed to turn black as they fell, and a certain exquisite cream kind with a slender red stem and bright scarlet leaves.

There were clumps of fairy bells, and all kinds of geraniums, and there were little trees of verbena and bluish lavender ☞

like bushes and a bed of pelagoniums with velvet eyes and leaves moths' wings. There was a bed of nothing but mignonette and another of nothing but pansies—borders of double and single daisies and all kinds of little tufty plants she had never seen before.

The red-hot pokers were taller than she; the Japanese sunflowers grew in a tiny jungle. She sat down on one of the box borders. By pressing hard at first it made a nice seat. But how dusty it was inside! Kezia bent down to look and sneezed and rubbed her nose.

And then she found herself at the top of the rolling grassy slope that led down to the orchard…She looked down at the slope a moment, then she lay down on her back, gave a squeak and rolled over and over into the thick flowery orchard grass. As she lay waiting for things to stop spinning, she decided to go up to the house and ask the servant girl for an empty match-box. She wanted to make a surprise for the grandmother…First she would put a leaf inside with a big violet lying on it, then she would put a very small white picotee, perhaps, on each side of the violet, and then she would sprinkle some lavender on the top, but not to cover their heads.

She often made these surprises for the grandmother, and they were always most successful.

"Do you want a match, my granny?"

"Why, yes, child, I believe a match is just what I'm looking for."

The grandmother slowly opened the box and came upon the picture inside.

"Good gracious, child! How you astonished me!"

"I can make her one every day here," she thought, scrambling up the grass on her slippery shoes.

But on her way back to the house she came to that island that lay in the middle of the drive, dividing the drive into two arms that met in front of the house. The island was made of grass banked up high. Nothing grew on the top except one huge plant with thick, gray-green, thorny leaves, and out of the middle there sprang up a tall stout stem. Some of the leaves of the plant were so old that they curled up in the air no longer; they turned back, they were split and broken; some of them lay flat and withered on the ground.

Whatever could it be? She had never seen anything like it before. She stood and stared. And then she saw her mother coming down the path.

"Mother, what is it?" asked Kezia.

Linda looked up at the fat swelling plant with its cruel leaves and fleshy stem. High above them, as though becalmed in the air, and yet holding so fast to the earth it grew from, it might have had claws instead of roots. The curving leaves seemed to be hiding something; the blind stem cut into the air as if no wind could ever shake it.

"That is an aloe, Kezia," said her mother.

"Does it ever have any flowers?"

"Yes, Kezia," and Linda smiled down at her, and half shut her eyes. "Once every hundred years."

I'll whisper it

A child that tells mother a secret is telling her how much she trusts her. This is how their relationship comes to be built on firm foundations. It will develop into one in which everything may be freely discussed, creating a really strong bond between them. Of course, it often happens that a child wants to whisper her secret just at the moment when mother needs to go off and do something, or the telephone is ringing, or the pan boiling over… but somehow the moment has to be grasped, in case it is lost forever.

Every secret is a huge issue to a child. Every secret matters. And every secret shared builds trust. The mother who starts off listening to how the rabbit kissed her little daughter will end up having much more complicated kissing issues confided to her later on. So it's really important to listen to the rabbit ones. When they reach their teens, children begin to fully appreciate their mother's listening ear and her discretion. The child who finds out her mother has told all her friends about her daughter's failed grades at school will soon stop telling her anything. The embarrassment and anger of a child betrayed by spilled secrets is hard to describe.

To keep children's secrets is to show them that they are worthy of respect, the root of all friendship. So they grow up to esteem themselves and others too, to care for another's innermost secrets as they do their own. This is a pretty wonderful gift, for there is one secret we all know, and that is that trust is a commodity quite difficult to find and terribly easy to lose.

Like mother, like daughter

Mother is the epitome of womanhood to all her children, but she's a special role model for her little girl. Watching, asking, and emulating, her daughter learns from her the art of being a woman, wife, and mother. At the kitchen table, in the garden, at the laundry basket, in the shop, or exploring mother's wardrobe, the lessons go on and on.

Adolescence may bring strife as the child struggles to form an identity that is separate from her mother. Shouting and sulking is often simply an indirectly expressed plea for understanding and, although it runs counter to female nature, often a mother's role is just to listen, not to talk!

It's a special moment when a young daughter watches, seemingly hypnotized, as mother dresses to go out, puts on her make-up, and arranges her hair. No one, she thinks, ever looked more beautiful. One day, she too will have mastered the mysteries of the dressing table: the magical lotions, creams, and perfume—so many ways to improve upon nature! Indeed, the entire cosmetics industry is built upon the perennial longing of women to transform themselves, to make themselves more alluring—an art as universal as it is effective. Make-up has often been called "war paint." If only all wars were as sweet!

But then comes that painful moment for a mother when she sees her own fading beauty in the mirror of her daughter's fresh young face:

"Thou art thy mother's glass, and she in thee

Calls back the lovely April of her prime."

And later still, a daughter will pause in her pastry-making; hesitate unconsciously while preparing the guestroom, pruning roses, or ironing a dress, assailed by some long-forgotten scent or sound, and find her heart suddenly flooded with the memory of how mother used to do it ...

The gentle touch

Brushing and braiding the hair has been an important ritual shared by mother and daughter over generations. These intimate moments have always been a good time to talk and exchange confidences. Girls used to be told that, to keep their hair healthy and shiny, they had to give it a hundred brush strokes a day. In the days before conditioners this served to distribute oils from the scalp through the hair, making it shine and keeping it from tangling. In the days before detergent shampoos, a dash of vinegar or beer was used in the final rinse to get rid of the last remnants of soap in the hair.

Grandmother rinsed her hair in rainwater to keep it soft, and she knew many herbal remedies to improve its beauty and sheen. Rosemary, lavender, and rosewater were all used as hair tonics, and a chamomile rinse enhanced the color of blond hair.

Now, as more girls are growing their hair long again, brushing is back in style again, along with all the yells and tangles! Smart mothers know that hair should not be combed or tugged when it is wet because it's at its most elastic then and very prone to damage. The chemicals in dyes and curling or straightening treatments are harmful—minimize attacks like this on the hair. Henna is a natural coloring that's been used for generations in Eastern cultures. It comes from the fragrant flowering oriental shrub *Lawsonia inermis*, which aptly enough is of the loosestrife family. A reddish-orange pigment is prepared from the leaves. This is made into a powder or paste that is applied to the hair and later rinsed off to reveal a beautifully natural chestnut color.

One at a time...

"Anyway, it was all her fault," says the bigger girl.

"No, it wasn't," whispers little sister.

"Yes, it was."

"She took the ball when it was my turn."

"No, I didn't (oh, she's such a telltale!). I'm allowed to have two goes if I won last time, aren't I, mother?"

Mother considers carefully. An error of judgment here will never be forgotten. "Your sister can have two goes too, because she's too young yet to know the rules."

"That's not fair!"

"Yes it is," squeaks the little one.

"No it isn't!"

"I want two goes too, because." Feeling exonerated, the little one abandons reason altogether.

Mother racks her brain to end the dispute once and for all. Brightly, she agrees: "That's a good idea. Then she gets more practice. And that's good because then one day she'll be able to win, too." There's certainly some fatal flaw in this argument but with a bit of luck it will go undetected in the highly charged atmosphere.

"She always gets her own way," retorts big sister sulkily.

"No, I don't. You get your own way, and more goes too."

The little one begins belatedly to cry. The big one regards her with scorn. What's that mother is saying? I have to show an example?

"Okay. Just this once, just because you don't really know how to play properly yet, I'll let you have two goes. But that's the last time!"

"Thank you, darling! That's great. Now go and play, both of you!"

The thing that impresses me most about America is the way parents obey their children.

EDWARD, DUKE OF WINDSOR

Pride and Prejudice

by

JANE AUSTEN

It is a truth universally acknowledged, that a single man in possession of a good fortune must be in want of a wife.

However little known the feelings or views of such a man may be on his first entering a neighbourhood, this truth is so well fixed in the minds of the surrounding families, that he is considered as the rightful property of some one or other of their daughters.

"My dear Mr. Bennet," said his lady to him one day, "have you heard that Netherfield Park is let at last?"

Mr. Bennet replied that he had not.

"But it is," returned she; "for Mrs. Long has just been here, and she told me all about it."

Mr. Bennet made no answer.

"Do not you want to know who has taken it?" cried his wife impatiently.

"You want to tell me, and I have no objection to hearing it."

This was invitation enough.

"Why, my dear, you must know, Mrs. Long says that Netherfield is taken by a young man of large fortune from the north of England; that he came down on Monday

Mr & Mrs Bennet

in a chaise and four to see the place, and was so much delighted with it that he agreed with Mr. Morris immediately; that he is to take possession before Michaelmas, and some of his servants are to be in the house by the end of next week."

"What is his name?"

"Bingley."

"Is he married or single?"

"Oh, single, my dear, to be sure! A single man of large fortune; four or five thousand a year. What a fine thing for our girls!"

"How so? how can it affect them?"

"My dear Mr. Bennet," replied his wife, "how can you be so tiresome! You must know that I am thinking of his marrying one of them."

"Is that his design in settling here?"

"Design! nonsense, how can you talk so! But it is very likely that he may fall in love with one of them, and therefore you must visit him as soon as he comes."

"I see no occasion for that. You and the girls may go, or you may send them by themselves, which perhaps will be still better; for, as you are as handsome as any of them, Mr. Bingley might like you the best of the party."

"My dear, you flatter me. I certainly have had my share of beauty, but I do not pretend to be anything extraordinary now. When a woman has five grown-up daughters, she ought to give over thinking of her own beauty."

"In such cases, a woman has not often much beauty to think of."

"But, my dear, you must indeed go and see Mr. Bingley when he comes into the neighbourhood."

"It is more than I engage for, I assure you."

"But consider your daughters. Only think what an establishment it would be for one of them. Sir William and Lady Lucas are determined to go, merely on that account; for in general, you know, they visit no newcomers. Indeed you must go, for it will be impossible for us to visit him, if you do not."

"You are over scrupulous, surely. I daresay Mr. Bingley will be very glad to see you; and I will send a few lines by you to assure him of my hearty consent to his marrying whichever he chooses of the girls; though I must throw in a good word for my little Lizzy."

"I desire you will do no such thing. Lizzy is not a bit better than the others: and I am sure she is not half so handsome as Jane, nor half so good-humoured as Lydia. But you are always giving her the preference."

"They have none of them much to recommend them," replied he: "they are all silly and ignorant like other girls; but Lizzy has something more of quickness than her sisters."

"Mr. Bennet, how can you abuse your own children in such a way? You take delight in vexing me. You have no compassion on my poor nerves."

A room of one's own

Children treasure the privacy of their own rooms and the only thing a mother needs to grasp when the proud moment of possession arrives is that she will not always be welcome there. This can be difficult to accept —especially when she often lacks any private space in the house herself. Having slaved over the curtains, the bedspread, and painting the walls, there she stands, wondering why she feels so foolish, outside a door marked "Private." Nothing for it but to knock and meekly ask, "Hello? Can I come in?" But this might not be the right moment to call, you understand. Inside, rehearsals are going on for LIFE.

Another useful lesson for mother is to never ever to get over-entangled (literally) in the great Clean-Up-Your-Room debate. This is a losing battle and everybody knows it. Children have their own logic in these things, and it's beyond the understanding of most adults. An exception was A. A. Milne, who wrote the *Winnie-the-Pooh* books to try to educate grown-ups. "One of the advantages of being disorderly," he explained, "is that one is constantly making exciting discoveries." He also remarked, for the edification of the same audience, that "Organizing is what you do before you do something, so that when you do it, it is not all mixed up."

Nowadays, many children not only have their own room in which to conduct a private experiment in chaos, but also a computer, television, CD player, and electronic games. "Knock at your peril, mother dear, within lies mortal danger; a gentle paradise for me, to you a den or stranger…"

Fun Project: 4
Fat cat doorstop

You will need

- Patterned fabric, about 12 × 20in/ 30 × 50cm
- Burlap, 2 pieces 4in/10cm wide and the width of a door
- Broad ribbon, about 1¼ yd/1.25m
- Poly stuffing or old tights or tee shirts
- Plain fabric, a scrap
- Paper, a scrap
- String or yarn, a scrap
- Darning needle
- Pins
- Sewing thread
- 2 buttons
- Pencil
- Scissors
- Pinking shears

Making the fat cat doorstop:

1 Make a paper pattern of a cat. Fold the fabric in half and pin on the paper pattern. Cut around the pattern with pinking shears.

2 On one cat shape, sew button eyes and glue on a fabric nose. Thread the darning needle with string or yarn and sew on a mouth and whiskers. Fray the ends of the whiskers.

3 Pin the two cat shapes together, right sides out. Sew them together using small running stitches. Leave a small gap in the base to push the stuffing through.

4 Stuff the cat with the poly stuffing, old tights, or tee shirt material. Use the end of a pencil to push the stuffing into the ears. Sew the gap closed.

5 Sew the strips of burlap together along three sides (two long and one short) to make a tail. Stuff the tail through the open end. Fray the bottom of it and sew the top end closed.

6 Sew the top of the tail to the side seam of the cat. Sew on a bow made with ribbon where the cat's neck would be.

To sew the mouth and whiskers in one go, start by pushing the needle into the fabric where the first whisker should go, come out at the mouth, make three stitches, and finish by bringing the needle out at the other whisker.

Cutting the fabric with pinking shears prevents it from fraying.

Make your stitches small and close together to prevent the stuffing from leaking out of the cat.

Run and get...

Money is a serious matter in family life, so being trusted by mother to run and get something from the store gives every child that first taste of adult responsibility. Mother takes the money from her purse and reminds the child that the change has to be exact and the things she wants accurately remembered. This is a great expression of mother's trust and makes the child feel truly grown-up.

The challenge for mother is to believe fully in her child. The challenge for the child is to dare for a while to abandon the internal world of dreams to cope with this foray into the big wide world. There is the street to negotiate, with its myriad little and large dangers, diversions, and distractions. Then there is the store itself: how to remain focused on the task in hand when shelves full of chocolate, candies, magazines, books, combs, hair things, toys, and trinkets beckon on every side?

At last the child finds what mother wants, pays for it, and even remembers to count the change. Back on the street outside, a surprising new feeling arrives—one of being older, wiser, and deeply content. So, that's cool! Junior carries the message home with pride. And there receives the change as a thank-you: the token of a true initiation.

SHOPPING SAVVY

Going shopping with mother never loses its charm. And it can also act as a subliminal teaching experience for a child: participating in choosing food and other necessities for the home is an excellent way to appreciate how much thought and organization goes into running and provisioning a household. That's the practical aspect.

The other side is the sheer thrill of being a consumer! A big store is an Aladdin's cave, full of all those enticing things you'd love to have, as well as the ones you actually need. Not so long ago. posters persuading us to buy were gentle in their prompting; today the art of seduction by advertisement is overwhelming.

So it's not surprising that children fall under the spell of consumerism and are constantly demanding things. And of course, delighting junior with something new is a pleasure for mother, too. Frequently, though, the modern mother finds herself under pressure from two sides—from all those seductive ads, and from her child's persistent chants of "I want!"

Kids today have significant economic influence—and those that don't have pester-power! Families with children are more likely to shop online and the majority allow their children to help them with this. Moreover, many children spend their money or buy and sell their things online.

So this is the birth of a shopping-savvy generation par excellence. It's a far cry from that traditional image of a mother and children filling their baskets with goodies from a neighborhood store. Can sitting in front of a computer really compare with the rush of adrenaline that comes from passing through the revolving doors of a big store? Surely not!

Trick or treat?

There's a real treat in store for mother at Halloween—making costumes for all her little wizards, witches, and wombats. What's it to be this year? Harry Potter lookalikes are still popular, but not that original anymore. Skeletons, ghosts, ghouls, goblins, and witches—well, okay.

But for older children, what about getting really wacky with The World's Most Popular Guy? All dressed up in his best, he can get a female friend to apply lots of lipstick and give him a few smacking kisses. Or he can look terrifying as a "Stepford wife" complete with hair rollers, facial mask, and mop. The Invisible Man can wear a tee shirt proclaiming who he is, plus the words, "So, you can see me? It's a terrible costume."

The Breath of Fresh Air wears all white, powders his or her face (flour will do), and carries a can of air freshener to spray now and then. A Bunch of Grapes is dressed in a green bodysuit covered with sewn-on green balloons. Clowns and magicians are easy with raccoon puppets, droopy paper flowers, and colored scarves de rigueur for both, and clothes as mismatched as possible for the clown.

The spooky festival of Halloween dates back to the Celts. Centuries later in Britain, it became linked to the bringing-in of the harvest at the end of October, after which the land lay "dead." The first day of November was called All Hallows Day, a solemn day of remembrance for dead relatives, when their souls found peace. But the night before was party night for all the departed of that year, when good and bad alike walked the earth for the last time. To scare away any evil spirits, people would dress up in disguise.

Christians celebrated this as All Souls Day, starting the custom of "souling." Beggars would go from house to house asking for a "soul cake" in return for praying for the souls of deceased relatives to ease their way to heaven. This was probably the beginning of "trick or treat." And the jack o'lantern comes from an Irish folktale about a wily old man who fell out of favor with both God and the Devil and was condemned to walk the earth forever with only a candle inside a pumpkin to light his way. The seeds of a pumpkin lantern, dried and threaded, make lovely jewelry, and you can make pumpkin pie from the flesh.

The famed escapist magician Houdini died on Halloween, October 31, 1926, still disbelieving in spirits of any sort. A big cardboard box makes a great "Houdini" costume. Rope could, at a stretch, also be considered a Houdini outfit, but make sure the wearer can get his hands free in time to grab the candy.

And for those mega-boring, responsible, old hippie-type people who go in for healthy treats, what about giving tissue-wrapped apples, tiny toys, pens, maybe some trading cards, or even some cool stickers? It's getting better. We'll be back with candy soon.

Fun Project: 5

Halloween jack o'lantern

You will need

- Pumpkin
- Craft knife (be careful)
- Spoon
- Pencil
- White cloves

- Dried orange slices
- Metal skewer
- Wool or twine, about
  1½ yards/1.5m
- Darning needle
- Tea light or votive candle

Making the jack o'lantern:

1 Cut a zigzag around the top of the pumpkin with the craft knife (an adult should help with this) and put this lid to one side. Scoop out the flesh and seeds of the pumpkin. Do not make the shell too thin. (Toast the seeds to eat, or save them to dry for bead jewelry.)

2 Draw eyes, nose, mouth, and star cheeks on the front of the pumpkin in pencil. Cut out the shapes with the craft knife. (This also needs adult help.) Press cloves into the cheeks. They'll smell lovely when the lantern is lit.

3 Push two holes in each side of the pumpkin with the skewer. Using the needle, thread each orange slice onto a piece of wool 1ft (30cm) long. Tie each piece of wool on the inside of the pumpkin, leaving the orange earring to dangle.

4 To make a handle, tie each end of a piece of wool, 30in (75cm) long, to the sides of the pumpkin, using the earring holes. Put the tea light inside the pumpkin and replace the lid.

For a really different lantern, let candlelight shine out through stars, moons, and tiny holes cut out all around the pumpkin.

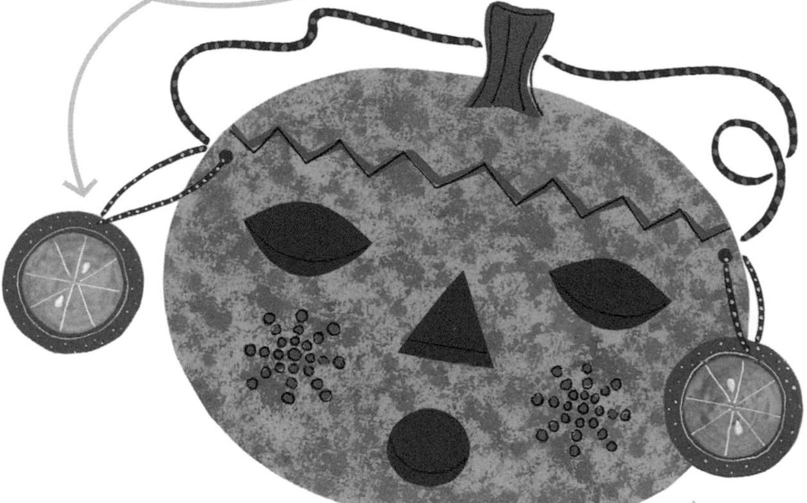
Cut slices of orange in advance and dry them slowly in a cool oven or over a radiator.
Make sure the earrings dangle on a level with the cheeks.

Halloween pumpkin pie

You simply can't have Halloween without pumpkins. Or pumpkin pie, for that matter. Canned pumpkin purée makes a yummy dish, but if you want to be really authentic, use the scooped-out flesh from your jack o'lantern (see Cook's Tip opposite.)

Preparation time: 5–25 minutes
Cooking time: 30–35 minutes

1 pre-baked 9in/23cm pastry shell
1¾ cups/675g pumpkin purée
3 carrots, halved lengthways and thinly sliced
2 eggs, beaten
Scant ½ cup/90g brown sugar
1 cup/250ml corn syrup
1 cup/250ml heavy cream
2 tsp/10ml ground cinnamon
1 tsp/5ml ground dried ginger
½ tsp/2.5ml ground nutmeg
1 tsp/5ml vanilla extract
Light cream, to serve

1 Put the pumpkin purée into a large mixing bowl.

2 Add the eggs, sugar, corn syrup, and cream to the pumpkin purée and mix well. Stir in the spices and vanilla extract.

3 Spoon the mixture into the pastry shell and bake in a preheated oven, 375°F/190°C/Gas 5, for 30–35 minutes until the filling is firm to the touch. Serve warm, with cold light cream.

Cook's tip

If you're using the scooped-out flesh of your jack o'lantern, you'll need a 2lb/900g pumpkin to yield 1½lb/675g pumpkin pulp. Cut the flesh into 2in/5cm pieces. Place the pieces in a pan and cover with water. Bring to a boil, then simmer for 15 minutes until tender. Drain the pumpkin very well, cool, and purée in a blender or food processor.

The A-Team

Mothers need fathers and fathers need mothers—they really do. Not just in the first place, but all the way through. And children need a mother-and-father team too. It's so much harder for them to learn the rules without the two sides, each with its distinctive and unique take on life and the world. Teamwork does not, of course, mean that people agree. If only. Sometimes they do. Maybe often! But where children are concerned, destabilizing disharmony has to be shelved. The ancient Chinese had the right idea with yin and yang: opposite and complementary elements, each one carrying the seed of the other in its deepest part.

So what is needed is what politicians are pleased to call a "solid coalition" between parents. A solid coalition means other people can't just come in and bust it up whenever they feel like it. Angelic infants have various ploys to achieve this end. One is to whisper lingeringly into one parent's ear the faults of the other, while sharing the same secrets with the other parent, in reverse. Children are past masters at this war game. And sadly enough, there are usually enough complicit parents to make it worthwhile. You only need two.

So if a healthy balance between male and female influence is to be maintained, infighting has to be hushed up in the interests of future generations. Each partner is then free to voice his or her wildly divergent vision and mission as far as the kids are concerned. That is, mother can say what a crazy idea she thinks it is to choose all science subjects in one semester, while father equally loudly expounds on the soundness of such a choice. Mother can spend the entire month's housekeeping on a prom dress for her daughter to wear just once, and father can go out and spend the same on yet another toolbox.

Variety, we all know, is of the essence in survival of the species, so it's quite essential that children grow up appreciating a bipolar view of the world. After all, they are all going to solidify in one direction or the other and need substantial role models. It's helpful for them to see how natural it is to belong to differing and delightfully opposing genders and that this is what makes life truly interesting. Usually children are at their most assertive just at the age when this is becoming patently obvious to them, so the timing around now of a resounding and unanimous *vive la différence* is often perfect.

Positive reinforcement of gender input is an art sometimes acquired under tricky circumstances, but is all the more precious for that. Keeping the unique attributes of the other side clearly in sight through all the noise and smoke of family life and not-quite-family life can be quite a challenge. But in the long-term, everybody definitely gains from remembering that two heads are better than one.

Wish you were here

Father, father where are you going?

WILLIAM BLAKE

Sometimes mother is left alone with the children, taking over the role of both parents for a while. When it's only for a limited time, this can be an interesting and enriching experience for all. Many mothers are surprised and delighted to see the different ways children have of taking on more responsibility. Often, a son will magically assume the role of "man about the house" and touching scenes will result. For example, he'll reassure mother that he's checked to see that the doors are locked at night. The girls, too, rally round to fill the gap, and the whole family may grow closer together. It's not unusual for a returning father to complain that there's no place for him anymore in his own home!

Sharing letters, telephone calls, and e-mails with father lets everyone feel involved and softens the pain of missing him. If he's away doing something exciting, everyone wants to be kept up to date with the adventure. Also, talking about him makes a difference and reading his words out loud can bring him back for a while.

More permanent absence through separation, divorce, or death, requires an even greater degree of communication between mother and children. Millions of children all over the world are brought up by a single parent, but this does not mean that the missing parent has to be banished from family conversation. For the children, perhaps the very opposite applies.

Within, the firelight's ruddy glow,
And childhood's nest of gladness.
The magic words shall hold thee fast:
Thou shalt not heed the raving blast.

LEWIS CARROLL

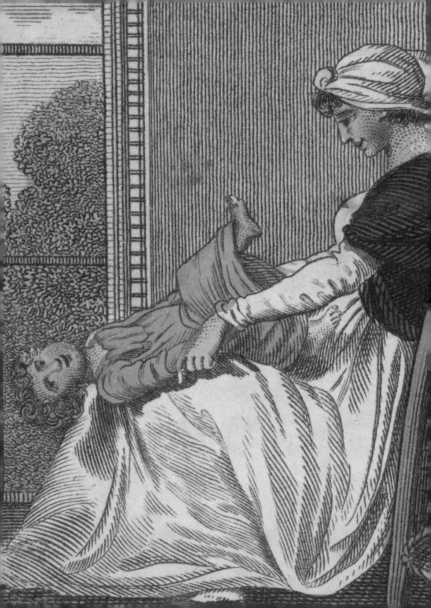

See-saw, Margery Daw

See-saw, Margery Daw,

Jacky shall have a new master.

He shall have but a penny a day,

Because he can't work any faster.

Toys, glorious toys!

Mothers tend to fall into two categories when it comes to buying toys for their children: one believes that they shouldn't have too many, and the other that they can never have enough. Most of us vacillate between the two, depending on how tired we are! Nearly all of us find today's toys too expensive. But every child loves visiting the toy department, so mother has to learn to enjoy it as well.

The best toys inspire a child to dream up games. Building blocks, dolls, trains, farmyards, little action figures, and even pistols and bows and arrows with accompanying cowboy hats and Indian feathers are all tried and tested favorites. Shrewd mothers keep a stash of old bits and pieces for children to use to "make things" to supplement their bought toys. This way, many a fine ocean-going liner, car, or robot has been constructed from discarded packaging, cardboard rolls, and boxes.

Custom-made toys have been found dating back to 4000 B.C. The ancient Chinese invented the yo-yo and roller skates. The first jigsaw puzzle was made in 1769. In 1895, the first bicycle was made, and in 1902, the teddy bear made his triumphant entrance, named after President "Teddy" Roosevelt. After this, toys really took off. Crayons appeared in 1903, Lionel trains in 1910, the trampoline in 1930, Monopoly in 1933, Scrabble in 1943, and the Frisbee in 1950. In 1949, Lego (Danish for "playing well") came on the scene, and in 1958, the hula hoop arrived—although children in ancient Egypt, Greece, Rome, and 14th-century England had played with these. Barbie was, in 1959, "every little girl's dream of the future." Ah! The future, as all mothers know, became entirely dominated by video games...

A PUPPET TO PLAY...

What mother has not paused while folding away the laundry to pull a sock over her hand, making an instant puppet for her child? In fact, the history of puppetry may be said to have begun with such a stocking or simple bag. The most basic puppet is a face drawn on the inside of the forefinger; the most complicated the marionette or puppet-on-a-string.

A child playing with puppets becomes both actor and audience in an enthralling drama—the appeal is so powerful that these acting-out games are played by children everywhere. The art of puppetry goes back a long way. Early Native American Indians used puppets in their corn festivals and ceremonial dances; and puppets were found in Athens in 421 B.C., from whence they made their way to India.

Mothers and children can enjoy hours of fun with the simplest of puppets—that little sock pulled over the hand can become a dog, a bird, or a funny person in the imagination of a child. And it makes it even more hilarious and wonderful if the puppet can talk, squeak, laugh, sing silly songs, behave outrageously, and dance around the room along with the child!

A truly appreciative child will break, lose, spoil, or fondle to death any really successful gift within a matter of minutes.

RUSSELL LYNES

First snow

The more it
snows,
(Tiddly Pom)
The more it goes

(Tiddly Pom)
The more it goes
(Tiddly Pom)
On snowing.

A. A. MILNE

It's a truly amazing moment when mother opens the front door and shows her child the first sight of a white world. Everything has been touched by a magic hand overnight, and all is sleeping beneath a white, downy quilt. There is a lovely quietness in the air. The gently drifting snowflakes fall into your hand—and then are gone. It's such a wonder how each one is so starry and so soft. Why can't we keep them forever? Why do they melt so fast?

You might see a robin redbreast hopping around, his tiny bright eyes looking for crumbs. Quick! Put on coats and wooly hat, scarf and mittens, warm woolen socks and then boots…Mother has to fetch a spade from the garden shed and help build a snowman. At last he stands proudly, with a carrot nose, stones for eyes, and an old pipe in his mouth. One of granddad's old hats goes on his head! Brrrrr! How cold my toes are.

Indoors again, mother makes steaming mugs of hot chocolate. Outside the window, the snowman shivers. Granddad tells how there used be ice flowers on the windows when he was young; and when you breathed on them, they would melt away. They were fairy flowers, left by the Ice Queen.

Mother Christmas

Christmas night. Everything is quiet, and mother is sitting down peacefully at last. All the excitement is over for another year. The turkey's eaten, the pie gone, and all that cooking is over. And this year she tells herself, yet again, how next year she'll do it differently—no huge roast, no long days of preparation, no shopping at the last minute. No, next year she'll do a cold buffet and that will be that. Except it won't, and she knows it. Next year will be just like this one. Only better.

Because next year they still won't have bought that fake Christmas tree that looks just like the real thing. They'll have the real thing again, only bigger, including the huge argument about when to buy it—too early and the needles fall off before Christmas Day, too late and there's no time to decorate it properly. And the argument about who's to help decorate it and when—and what with; who in heaven's name put the things away last year, and why did he—it must have been him—stash them away at the back of the attic? Has he no sense? Couldn't he have known Christmas would come around again so soon? What does he mean: a year's a long time? And the tears because the baby helped mother make the fairy for the top, so all the older ones feel free to jeer at it and say how it doesn't look a bit like a fairy, or an angel, or even a weird bird.

And next year everyone will love their presents even more because she'll make an advance list, noting down every time someone mentions something they want, and then she'll start the shopping in around August or September. And when people ask her what she wants she'll really THINK about it, so next year she doesn't get quite so many shower gels and soaps-on-a-rope and Chinese recipe books and gift books such as this year's: *A Mother's Guide to Surviving Christmas* ...

Yes, that's right. Next year she won't overcook the vegetables. Or put the turkey in just an hour or so too late, or drink that last cocktail at the neighbors' house, because those last two are connected. Those Christmas morning parties next door are just FATAL. And next year the consommé will be perfect and so will the sorbet, and she won't insist that everyone eat Christmas fruitcake. So then they won't all tell her in unison how they feel nauseous. And the brandy she pours over it will flame. That's it! The brandy will flame blue, and then it will be really perfect ...

"What a perfect Christmas, darling!"

Who said that?

"You are truly wonderful!"

Oh. Do you really think so? Well, thank you. Thank you very much!

Gingerbread Christmas cookies

Makes 30 to 40

3 cups/350g all-purpose flour
1 tbsp/15ml baking powder
2 tsp/10ml ground ginger
½ tsp/2.5ml ground allspice
¼ cup/60ml molasses
¼ cup/60ml light corn syrup
¾ stick/75g butter
3 tbsp/45ml packed dark
   brown sugar
1 egg, beaten

Frosting
1¼ cups/155g powdered sugar
1 tbsp/15ml lemon juice

1 Lightly grease two baking sheets. Sift the flour, baking powder, and spices into a bowl.

2 Place the molasses, corn syrup, butter, and brown sugar in a small pan and heat gently, stirring until well combined.

3 Let cool slightly, then beat in the egg. Pour into the dry ingredients and mix to form a firm dough. Let rest for a few minutes, then knead gently until smooth.

4 Preheat the oven to 350°F/180°C/Gas 4. On a lightly floured surface, roll out the dough to ¼in/6mm thick and cut out cookies with cookie cutters. Place on the baking sheets and bake until crisp and golden, 10 to12 minutes. Let cool on the baking sheets for 2 to 3 minutes, then transfer to a wire rack to cool completely.

5 To make the frosting, sift the powdered sugar into a bowl, add the lemon juice, and mix until smooth. Spread or pipe over the cookies. Let stand until the frosting has set, 1 to 2 hours. Store in an airtight container for up to two weeks.

Cook's Tip
To hang the cookies as decorations, make a small hole at the top of each cookie with a skewer before baking. Reopen the hole as soon as the cookies come out of the oven. When the cookies are cool, thread a length of ribbon through the hole and tie the ends.

Fun Project: 6
Christmas tree fairy

You will need

- Thin colored poster paper, about 16in/ 40cm square (body)
- Colored paper, a small sheet (head)
- Silver poster board or paper, about 6 x 12in/ 15 x 30cm (wings)
- 4 popsicle sticks
- Assorted tiny beads, buttons, sequins
- Star stickers
- Yellow, orange, or brown tissue paper, thin strips
- Felt scrap

- Cocktail stick
- Dinner plate
- Gold thread
- Embroidery thread
- Embroidery needle
- Felt-tip pens
- Sticky tape
- Scissors
- Pinking shears
- Glue

Making the fairy

1 Cut a semicircle from the poster paper with the pinking shears, drawing around the dinner plate. Make the semicircle into a cone and tape it in place. Cut off the top of the cone.

2 Cover two popsicle-stick arms with folded colored paper to make the sleeves, leaving "hands" peeking out. Glue the arms onto the back of the cone.

3 Fold the silver poster paper in half. Draw a wing on the paper, with the fold in the middle. Cut out the wing and open it. Decorate it with stars and sequins. Glue it to the back of the cone.

4 Cut a head and neck from poster paper. Draw on a nose and mouth. Glue on bead or button eyes and tissue paper hair. Thread beads or sequins together for a halo and glue them in place. Tape the neck inside the cone.

5 Decorate two popsicle-stick legs with colored felt-tip pens. Glue on two felt shoes. For the bows, make a stitch with embroidery thread, knot the ends, and fray. Glue the legs inside the front of the cone.

6 For the fairy's wand, glue one end of a length of gold thread to the tip of the cocktail stick. Wind the thread around the stick, covering it. Glue a star or sequin to the top. Decorate the fairy's dress with sequins and stars.

Glue the wand onto the popsicle-stick hand.

You can sew the button or bead eyes onto the fairy's face if you wish.

Make the fairy's dress and wings sparkle with lots of shiny stars and sequins.

Stitch a short piece of colored raffia onto the shoes and unravel to make a different sort of bow.

289

The great room was entirely changed; for now it looked like a garden, or one of the fairy scenes children love, where in-doors and out-of-doors are pleasantly combined.

LOUISA MAY ALCOTT, *JACK AND JILL*

Party animals

The main thing about a party is that mother and child both enjoy it. So out with worry, exhaustion, stress, and over-excitement, and in with calm, relaxed assurance that you're going to give the best party in town and one they'll never forget. And by remembering that children remember what they did at a party and not what they ate, what the paper napkins looked like, or how clean the house was, and because you don't need to invite the adults, you can save yourself a whole lot of heartache, headache, and backache, too.

Best party times are 1 to 3 P.M. or 2 to 4 P.M.; no meal has to be served. Little ones won't need a nap if you party from 10 A.M. until 11.30 A.M. The number of invitations can follow a frugal rule: as many as the child's age, or maybe one or two more. Siblings don't have to be asked, and neither do parents. They enjoy the break. The birthday boy or girl can choose a theme and make activity stations: blocks at one, Play-Do at another, and so on.

It's really nice to keep party favors modest and theme them with the party. Kids can take home a little flowerpot with seeds from a "garden party," or a small bag of modeling clay from an "art party." They can make their favors during the party, because the best parties are busy ones. Lots of outdoor activities can be fun if the backyard is big enough. A treasure hunt is irresistible, and the "treasure" can be the finders' favors.

If there are organized games, there must never be losers. Losing is no fun. Grown-ups always have trouble letting children win—big babies—but in children's games there is always room for another winner; even the one who's "out" in musical chairs can be in charge of the music and come back in again next round. Other good games are Catch the Balloon, where one child stands in the middle of the circle and throws a balloon into the air while calling out the name of another child, who has to catch it before it hits the ground. If it does, that child goes in the middle. Another is Poor Kitty, where one child is blindfolded in the center of a ring of very quiet children. The blindfolded one moves out into the ring and when he reaches someone, that child meows and says, "Poor kitty," and the other has to identify him or her. If he does so correctly, this "kitty" goes into the middle.

There are some wonderful party themes. How about the Alphabet Party, Backwards Party, Bug Party, Color Party, Dance Party, Fear Factor Party, Gymnastics Party, Mermaid Party, Sixties Party, Splash in the Backyard Party, the Sweet Sixteen Party, the Under the Sea Party, and Western Party. The Safari Sleepover Party—bring your own tent. Or the one where everyone keeps it a surprise what they're coming dressed up as, and a prize button goes to the scariest, funniest, silliest, noisiest, brightest ... whatever.

Then there's the sleepover...

Often, a party is followed by a sleepover. The first tests a mother's powers of invention; the second her endurance. Both are pretty powerful stuff and luckily only come up about once a year for each child. A birthday party is most cool when it has a theme. This means dreaming one up and then trying to imagine how on earth to execute it. For example, a gothic party for teenagers might mean painting all the walls black, taking all the light bulbs out, and most significantly, your going out for the evening, dressed in black. This will be the plea, anyway, backed up by the insistence that this is what ALL the other parents do. It's funny how fast children age when it suits them. However, this sort of ultimatum ultimately comes down to a simple choice between your furniture and a fairly temporary lapse in good relations with your child. So it's quite straightforward.

Exhausted with the creative effort of thinking up themes—books, films, star signs, seasons, videos, bands, festivals—and dressing the child, the house, and the table accordingly, mother is now faced with the sleepover. This begins with a whole roomful of kids in various stages of undress, all asking where they are to sleep—while none has the slightest intention of doing so. Finally they are all lying down, more or less. But you can tell from the breathing that it won't be for long.

When you next look in, they are all in one another's sleeping bags or beds and have found or smuggled in something more to eat. This is a sort of ongoing midnight feast accompanied by giggling, beginning at about bedtime and going on until they mercifully fall asleep, around four in the morning. It's impossible for anyone in the house to sleep during this time because of the noise of bags of potato chips being opened and thrown around, chocolate wrappers, ditto, and children generally falling over one another in fits of hysteria. At last it is quiet, and you too may sleep, perchance to dream of clearing up the mess tomorrow. Two lots of detritus are involved—one official, the other all sorts of unspeakable bits and pieces that have found their way into parts of the bedroom never before discovered.

But behold, there is also a secret place in every mother's heart where she cherishes these occasions. For they touch upon some deeply hidden and denied desire—we all have these, apparently—to be a true earth mother, to hold a hundred children in our arms, to feed, warm, and water them. To transport them to fairy wonderlands where childhood goes on forever and the world is as they imagine it, where day is night and night is day and everything may be eaten and all will be forgiven them. Where we don't mind what they do because we are their mother. And we'll always clear up afterwards. Children have long, long memories. Silly us!

Watch the birdie!

Those fun snapshots you took during your child's first summer vacation will build lasting memories. In years to come, you may suddenly stumble upon an old picture album and spend hours dreaming of those exciting, long-ago days!

The devoted mother begins a Baby Book during her pregnancy and somehow finds the time to keep it up from birth all through her child's early years. (How else will she one day share her pride and joy with her child's new sweetheart?) A typical album may contain everything from prenatal scan pictures to the birth announcement and very first baby pictures, handprinted birthday party invitations, first drawings and essays, notes of sporting achievements. But the real memories will be preserved magically in the photographs.

The history of family photography began only some 150 years ago, with the introduction of the box camera by George Eastman in 1888. Victorian mothers popularized formal portraits of their children, each stiffly posed, dressed in their Sunday best and clutching a flower or beloved toy. These portraits were proudly placed in ornate frames and displayed in the living room or carried as a keepsake with a lock of hair in a locket around the neck.

The 19th-century photographer used many devices to try to win and keep the attention of his subject while the camera took its long exposure and he was hidden beneath the black, light-excluding cloth. One such device was a little brass bird that sat on the top of the camera, sometimes even tweeting and fluttering its tail at the squeeze of an air bulb in the photographer's hand. This is the origin of the command "Watch the birdie!" and it's still in faithful use today.

Alice's Adventures in Wonderland

by

LEWIS CARROLL

"Please would you tell me," said Alice, a little timidly, for she was not quite sure whether it was good manners for her to speak first, "why your cat grins like that?"

"It's a Cheshire cat," said the Duchess, "and that's why. Pig!"

She said the last word with such sudden violence that Alice quite jumped; but she saw in another moment that it was addressed to the baby, and not to her, so she took courage, and went on again:—

"I didn't know that Cheshire cats always grinned; in fact, I didn't know that cats COULD grin."

"They all can," said the Duchess; "and most of 'em do."

"I don't know of any that do," Alice said very politely, feeling quite pleased to have got into a conversation.

"You don't know much," said the Duchess; "and that's a fact."

Alice did not at all like the tone of this remark, and thought it would be as well to introduce some other subject of conversation. While she was trying to fix on one, the cook took the cauldron of soup off the fire, and at once set to work throwing everything within her reach at the Duchess and the baby—the fire-irons came first; then followed a shower of saucepans, plates, and dishes. The Duchess took no notice of them even when they hit her; and the baby was howling so much already, that it was quite impossible to say whether the blows hurt it or not.

"Oh, PLEASE mind what you're doing!" cried Alice, jumping up and down in an agony of terror. "Oh, there goes his PRECIOUS nose"; as an unusually large saucepan flew close by it, and very nearly carried it off.

"If everybody minded their own business," the Duchess said in a hoarse growl, "the world would go round a deal faster than it does."

"Which would NOT be an advantage," said Alice, who felt very glad to get an opportunity of showing off a little of her knowledge. "Just think of what work it would make with the day and night! You see the earth takes twenty-four hours to turn round on its axis—"

"Talking of axes," said the Duchess, "chop off her head!"

Alice glanced rather anxiously at the cook, to see if she meant to take the hint; but the cook was busily stirring the soup, and seemed not to be listening, so she went on again: "Twenty-four hours, I THINK; or is it twelve? I—"

"Oh, don't bother ME," said the Duchess; "I never could abide figures!" And with that she began nursing her child again, singing a sort of lullaby to it as she did so, and giving it a violent shake at the end of every line:

"Speak roughly to your little boy, And beat him when

he sneezes: He only does it to annoy, Because he knows it teases."

CHORUS.

(In which the cook and the baby joined):—

"Wow! wow! wow!"

While the Duchess sang the second verse of the song, she kept tossing the baby violently up and down, and the poor little thing howled so, that Alice could hardly hear the words:—

"'I speak severely to my boy, I beat him when he sneezes; For he can thoroughly enjoy, The pepper when he pleases!'"

CHORUS.

"Wow! wow! wow!"

"Here! you may nurse it a bit, if you like!" the Duchess said to Alice, flinging the baby at her as she spoke. "I must go and get ready to play croquet with the Queen," and she hurried out of the room. The cook threw a frying-pan after her as she went out, but it just missed her.

Alice caught the baby with some difficulty, as it was a queer-shaped little creature, and held out its arms and legs in all directions, "just like a star-fish," thought Alice. The poor little thing was snorting like a steam-engine when she caught it, and it kept doubling itself up and straightening itself out again, so that altogether, for the first minute or two, it was as much as she could do to hold it.

As soon as she had made out the proper way of nursing it, (which was to twist it up into a sort of knot, and then keep tight hold of its right ear and left foot, so as to prevent its undoing itself), she carried it out into the open air. "IF I don't take this child away with me," thought Alice, "they're sure to kill it in a day or two: wouldn't it be murder to leave it behind?" She said the last words out loud, and the little thing grunted in reply (it had left off sneezing by this time). "Don't grunt," said Alice; "that's not at all a proper way of expressing yourself."

The baby grunted again, and Alice looked very anxiously into its face to see what was the matter with it. There could be no doubt that it had a VERY turn-up nose, much more like a snout than a real nose; also its eyes were getting extremely small for a baby: altogether Alice did not like the look of the thing at all. "But perhaps it was only sobbing," she thought, and looked into its eyes again, to see if there were any tears.

No, there were no tears. "If you're going to turn into a pig, my dear," said Alice, seriously, "I'll have nothing more to do with you. Mind now!" The poor little thing sobbed again (or grunted, it was impossible to say which), and they went on for some while in silence.

Alice was just beginning to think to herself, "Now, what am I to do with this creature when I get it home?" when it grunted again, so violently, that she looked down into its face in some alarm. This time there could be NO mistake about it: it was neither more nor less than a pig, and she felt that it would be quite absurd for her to carry it further.

Picture Credits